Python Programming Bible

3 in 1

The Complete Crash Course to Learn and Explore Python beyond the Basics.

*Including Examples and Practical Exercises to Master Python **from Beginners to Pro**.*

By

James P. Meyers

Table of Contents

Introduction to Python **15**
What is Python? 15
Brief history and development of Python 16
Features and strengths of Python 16
Why learn Python? 17
Real-world applications of Python 17
Career opportunities with Python: 18
Installing Python 18
Windows: 19
macOS: 19
Linux: 20
Configuring the Python Environment: 20
Python Development Environments 21
Choosing the Right IDE for Your Needs 22

BOOK 1 .... **25**

Chapter 1: Basic Concepts **26**
Data Types 26
Numeric Types 27
Boolean Type 28
Dynamic Typing 30
Variables 31
Assignment 32
Naming rules 32
Dynamic typing 33
Operators 33
Arithmetic Operators 34
Comparison Operators 35
Logical Operators 36
Bitwise Operators 36
Basic Data Structures 37
Lists 38
Tuples 38

Dictionaries 39
Control Flow 40
for Loops 40
while Loops 43
Loop Control Statements 45
Python Conditional Statements 47
If Statement 47
If-Else Statement 48
else: 49
Elif Statement 49
Nested If Statement 50
One Line Conditional Statements 50
Multiple Conditions in If Statement 51
Exercises 51

Functions and Modules 53

Functions and Parameters 53
Defining and Calling Functions 53
Positional and Keyword Arguments 53
User Defined vs Built in Functions 54
Function Arguments 56
Docstrings 60
Exercises 62
Return Statement 62
Returning Values 64
Multiple Return Values 64
Built-in Functions 65
Importing Modules 66
Overview of Python Modules 66
Importing Modules in Your Code 67
Creating and Using Your Own Modules 67
Creating a Custom Python Module 67
Using a Custom Python Module 68
Organizing Your Code with Modules 68
Practical Exercise: Building a Simple Calculator 69
Practical Exercise: Creating and Manipulating Data Structures 70

Chapter 2: Input and Output **71**
Standard Input/Output 71
Basic input/output with Python 72
Reading and writing to the console 72
Reading and Writing Files 73
Reading text and binary files with Python 73
Writing data to files 74
Error Handling 74
Handling exceptions with try/except blocks 75
Raising your own exceptions 75
Practical Exercise: File Manipulation and Error Handling 76

Chapter 3: Object-Oriented Programming **78**
Classes and Objects 78
Methods and Attributes 79
Inheritance 81
The Benefits of Inheriting Properties and Methods From Parent Classes 81
Creating child classes 82
Polymorphism 82
Using polymorphism in Python 83
Polymorphism in Inheritance 83
Overriding Methods 83
Practical Exercise: Building a Class Hierarchy 85

Chapter 4: Advanced Topics **87**
Regular Expressions 87
Overview of Regular Expressions: 88
Using Regular Expressions in Python: 88
Lambda Functions 89
Introduction to Lambda Functions: 90
List Comprehensions 91
Creating Lists with List Comprehensions: 91
Advanced List Comprehension Techniques: 92
Decorators 92
Overview of Decorators in Python: 93

Creating and Using Decorators: 93
Generators 94
Overview of Generators in Python: 94
Creating and Using Generators: 95

BOOK 2 **97**

Chapter 1: Python Libraries and Applications **98**

Python Standard Libraries with Codes 98
math - Mathematical Functions 99
datetime - Date and Time Handling 99
random - Generate Pseudo-random Numbers 100
statistics - Mathematical Statistic Functions 100
string - String Operations 101
re - Regular Expression Operations 101
collections - Container Data Types 102
NumPy 103
Overview of NumPy: 103
Using NumPy for numerical computations: 104
NumPy Arrays 105
NumPy Array Attributes 106
Array Indexing 107
Array Operations 108
NumPy Exercises 110
Pandas 110
Overview of Pandas 110
Using Pandas for data manipulation and analysis: 114
Pandas Series 115
Pandas DataFrames 116
Dataframe Indexing 117
Handling Missing Data 118
Dataframe Operations 118
Data Aggregation 119
Pandas Exercises 120
Matplotlib 121
Overview of Matplotlib: 122
Creating data visualizations with Matplotlib: 122

Basic XY Plot ... 123
Bar Charts ... 124
Histograms ... 125
Scatter Plots ... 125
Figures and Subplots ... 126
Matplotlib Exercises ... 127
Flask ... 127
Building web applications with Flask ... 127
Overview of Flask ... 128
Basic Application ... 129
Request and Response ... 129
Application Structure ... 130
Database Integration ... 131
Flask Exercises ... 132
Django ... 132
Overview of Django ... 132
Building web applications with Django ... 133
Project Setup ... 134
Django Apps ... 135
Models and Database ... 136
Views and Templates ... 136
Admin Interface ... 138
Django Exercises ... 138
Practical Exercise: Data Analysis with NumPy and Pandas ... 139
The Dataset ... 139
Problem Statement ... 140
Setup ... 140
Data Cleansing ... 142
Exploratory Analysis ... 143
Key Takeaways ... 145
Chapter 2: Working with APIs ... 146
What are APIs? ... 146
Types of APIs ... 147
HTTP Requests and Responses ... 148
Overview of HTTP protocol ... 148
Sending and receiving HTTP requests with Python ... 148

JSON Data Format ... 149
Introduction to JSON ... 149
Parsing and creating JSON data in Python ... 149
Accessing APIs with Python ... 150
Using the Requests library to access APIs ... 150
Authentication with APIs ... 151
Examples of Popular APIs ... 153
X (Twitter) API ... 153
OpenWeatherMap API ... 153
Google Maps API ... 154
Exercises ... 154

Chapter 3: Data Analysis and Visualization ... 155

Reading Data with Pandas ... 155
Importing data into Pandas ... 157
Working with different data formats ... 158
Data Cleaning and Preparation ... 158
Handling missing data ... 159
Data normalization and scaling ... 159
Exploratory Data Analysis ... 160
Summary statistics and visualizations ... 161
Data profiling and exploration techniques ... 161
Visualizing Data with Matplotlib and Seaborn ... 161
Creating charts and graphs with Matplotlib ... 163
Using Seaborn for advanced visualization ... 163
Basic Statistical Analysis with Python ... 163
Descriptive Statistics ... 164
Hypothesis Testing ... 165
Exercises ... 166

Chapter 4: Machine Learning with Python ... 167

Overview of Machine Learning ... 167
Types of Machine Learning Algorithms ... 168
Supervised and Unsupervised Learning ... 168
Supervised Learning ... 168
Unsupervised Learning ... 170
Difference between Supervised and Unsupervised Learning ... 171

Scikit-Learn Library 172
Using Scikit-Learn for machine learning tasks 172
Examples of using Scikit-Learn for machine learning tasks 173
Common Machine Learning Algorithms 174
Applications of Machine Learning in Python 176
Sample Code Snippets 178

Chapter 5: Web Scraping with Python 182

What is Web Scraping? 182
How to Use Python for Web Scraping 183
Requests Library 183
BeautifulSoup Library 184
Scraping Data from Websites 184
Step 1: Send a GET Request 184
Step 2: Parse the HTML 185
Step 3: Extract Data 185
Data Extraction and Cleaning 186
Regular Expressions 186
String Manipulation 186
Practical Exercise - Creating a Simple Web Scraper 187
Setup 187
Making Requests 188
Parsing Content 188
Extracting Data 189
Analysis in Pandas 189

Chapter 6: Data Science with Python 191

Introduction to Data Science 191
Working with Data Frames in Python 192
Data Visualization with Matplotlib and Seaborn 193
Exploratory Data Analysis and Statistical Analysis 194
Linear and Logistic Regression Analysis 195
Linear Regression with Scikit-learn 196
Logistic Regression with Scikit-learn 197

Chapter 7: Web Development with Python 199

Introduction to Web Development with Python 199

Creating Dynamic Websites Using Flask and Django 200
Building Web Applications with Python 202

Chapter 8: Testing and Debugging in Python 205

Why Testing and Debugging is Important 205
Types of Testing in Python 206
Unit Testing with Pytest 207
Debugging Techniques in Python 208
Profiling Python Code 209
Practical Exercise - Test-Driven Development (TDD) 210
What is TDD 210
Project Setup 210
First Test 211
Expanding Tests 211

Chapter 9: Best Practices and Code Optimization 213

Writing Clean and Readable Code 213
Use Descriptive Names 213
Style Guide Conventions 214
Modularize Code 214
Use Code Comments 215
Validate Input Data 216
Handle Errors 216
Adopt Linting and Formatting Tools 217
Follow DRY Principle 218
Limit Line Length 219
Performance Optimization Tips 220
Leverage Vectorization 220
Use Generators for Lazy Evaluation 221
Profile Bottlenecks 222
Practical Exercise: Code Review and Optimization 223
Code Overview 223
Refactoring Goals 223
Optimization Goals 223
Setup 224
Assess Bugs 224
Improve Style and Naming 224

Restructure and Encapsulate 225
Profile to Optimize 225

Chapter 10: Networking with Python 227

Introduction to Networking in Python 227
Basic Networking Concepts 228
Socket Programming with Python 228
Client-Server Communication in Python 230
Networking Libraries in Python (e.g. Twisted, Scapy) 231
Exercises 233
Exercises for Socket Programming with Python 233
Exercises for Client-Server Communication in Python 235
Exercises for Networking Libraries in Python (Twisted and Scapy) 235

Chapter 11: Game Development with Python 237

Introduction to Game Development with Python 237
Pygame library for Game Development 238
Creating Games with Python 241
Physics Simulation in Python Game Development 241
Game Design Principles and Strategies 243
Exercises 244
Exercise 1: Create a Simple Pong Game with Pygame 244
Exercise 2: Add Sprite Animations to a Pygame Game 244
Exercise 3: Implement Collision Detection in a 2D Platformer 244

Chapter 12: Cybersecurity with Python 245

Introduction to Cybersecurity with Python 245
Cryptography and Encryption in Python 246
Network Security with Python 247
Web Security with Python 249
Threat Detection and Response with Python 250
Exercises 251

Chapter 13: Big Data with Python 253

Introduction to Big Data and Python 253
Processing Big Data with Python 254

Working with Hadoop and Spark using Python 256
Storing and Managing Big Data with Python 258
Data Visualization and Analysis for Big Data with Python 259
Exercises 261

Chapter 14: Natural Language Processing with Python 263

Introduction to Natural Language Processing: 264
Text Pre-Processing and Cleaning with Python 265
Sentiment Analysis with Python 267
Named Entity Recognition with Python 268
Topic Modeling with Python 270
Exercises 272

BOOK 3 275

Chapter 1: Deep Learning with Python 276

Introduction to deep learning 276
Neural network basics 277
Keras library for deep learning with Python 278
Build a simple neural network to classify handwritten digits using MNIST dataset: 279
Build a CNN to classify CIFAR-10 images: 280
Fine-tune ResNet model for custom image classification: 280
Build LSTM network to generate text: 281
Sentiment analysis with LSTM: 282
Object detection with YOLO: 282
Image captioning with CNN-RNN: 283
Convolutional neural networks for image processing 284
Recurrent neural networks for natural language processing 284
Exercises 286

Chapter 2: Cloud Computing with Python 287

Introduction to Cloud Computing with Python 287
Cloud Computing Platforms (e.g. AWS, Google Cloud, Azure) 289
Managing Cloud Infrastructure with Python 289
Deploying Python Applications to the Cloud 290
Big Data Processing in the Cloud with Python 291

Exercises....292

Chapter 3: GUI Programming with Python 293

Tkinter library for GUI programming with Python....295
Building desktop applications with Python....296
Designing user interfaces with Python....296
Event-driven programming in GUI programming with Python....297
Practical Exercise: Developing a Simple GUI Application....298
Import Tkinter and create the main window object....298
Create input fields to get contact details from the user....298
Add labels to identify each input field....298
Add a submit button to save the contact....298
Save the contact details in a dictionary on submit button click.299
Display the contact details when a name is entered in a search field....299
Exercises....299

Chapter 4: Mobile App Development with Python 301

Introduction to Mobile App Development with Python....301
Kivy Library for Mobile App Development with Python....302
Building Cross-Platform Mobile Apps with Python....302
User Interface Design for Mobile Apps with Python....303
Mobile App Deployment with Python....303
Exercises....305

Chapter 5 : Real-world Projects and Case Studies....306

Developing a Web Application....306
Flask Overview....307
Project Setup....307
Defining Routes....308
Rendering Templates....309
Handling Forms....310
Database Integration....311
Deployment....311
Data Analysis and Visualization Project....312
Project Overview....312
Loading Data....313

Exploring Data 313
Data Cleaning 314
Feature Engineering 314
Model Training 315
Data Visualization 316
Automation Scripts and Tools 316
Web Scraping 317
File Processing 318
Excel Automation 319
Email Scripts 319
Practical Exercise: Building a Project from Scratch 320
Project Overview 320
Set Up Environment 321
Database Model 321
Database Setup 322
Define CLI Interface 322
Integrate Database 323
Run the CLI 324

Chapter 6: Future Work and Next Steps 325

Review of Python Basics 325
Tips for Continued Learning and Practice 326
Future Directions and Applications for Python 328
Applications of Python in different fields: 328
Appendix: Python Reference 329
Python Version 329
Syntax 330
Data Types 330
Variables 331
Operators 331
String Methods 332
Date and Time 332
File Handling 333
Exception Handling 334
Exercises 335

Conclusion 337

Introduction to Python

In recent times, Python has gained popularity as a high-level programming language due to its simplicity, versatility, and power. It is used for a lot of different things, like building websites, doing scientific computing, and making artificial intelligence. In this chapter, we'll show you what Python is and what it can do for you. Furthermore, we will provide guidance on how to install Python and establish a suitable development environment.

What is Python?

Guido van Rossum developed Python, a general-purpose programming language, in the late 1980s. Python's design philosophy emphasizes simplicity, code readability, and ease of use. The language is open-source, allowing free usage and contribution by all.

The versatility of Python is one of its major strengths. It can be applied to various applications, including web development, scientific computing, and artificial intelligence. Companies like Google, Facebook, Dropbox, and many others make use of it.

Python is also known for its clear and concise syntax. Python uses indentation to denote block structure, making code more readable and comprehensible. Furthermore, Python has a vast and active developer community that contributes to its advancement and creates additional libraries and tools that enhance its functionalities.

Brief history and development of Python

Python was initially released in 1991 and has since undergone numerous significant updates and versions. The language has evolved to become a versatile tool for software development, scientific computing, and data analysis.

In the early 2000s, Python's powerful libraries, such as NumPy, SciPy, and Matplotlib, helped it become very popular in scientific computing. When Django, a web framework for building web apps, came out, it made the language popular in web development as well.

Currently, Python is among the most widely used programming languages globally, serving various purposes such as scientific computing, data analysis, web development, artificial intelligence, and machine learning, to name a few.

Features and strengths of Python

Python's simplicity, readability, and user-friendliness are some of its defining features and strengths. Some of its notable characteristics include:

- Easy-to-learn syntax: Python's simple and uncluttered syntax is easy to learn and understand, making it an excellent language for novice programmers.
- Large standard library: Python comes with a vast standard library that includes modules for various functions such as file I/O, networking, and database operations, among others. This feature makes it easy to write complex applications without having to start from scratch.

- Cross-platform compatibility: Python can operate on multiple platforms, including Windows, macOS, and Linux, among others. This makes it highly adaptable, allowing users to develop and execute programs across multiple operating systems.
- Object-oriented programming support: Python supports object-oriented programming (OOP), a programming approach that allows developers to write modular and reusable code, reducing the amount of time spent on writing repetitive code.

Python's versatility stems from its broad range of applications. Developers can use Python to build websites, perform scientific computations, conduct data analysis, and implement artificial intelligence and machine learning solutions, among other applications.

Why learn Python?

Python is a widely-used programming language that has numerous applications. Acquiring proficiency in Python can lead to vast career prospects and assist in resolving intricate problems. Here are some of the reasons why you should consider learning Python:

Real-world applications of Python

Python is applied in various practical, real-world scenarios, ranging from web development, data analysis to scientific computing, with companies like Google, Facebook, Dropbox, among others, utilizing it. Here are some common areas where Python is frequently used:

- Web development: Python frameworks, including Flask and Django, are used to build web applications.
- Data analysis and visualization: Python has an array of libraries and tools, such as NumPy, Pandas, and Matplotlib, which facilitate data analysis and visualization.

- Scientific computing: Python is widely applied in scientific computing applications, such as in the fields of physics, biology, and chemistry.
- Artificial intelligence and machine learning: Python has multiple libraries and tools for artificial intelligence and machine learning, including TensorFlow and PyTorch.
- Automation and scripting: System administrators and testers often use Python to write scripts and automate tasks.

Career opportunities with Python:

Acquiring Python proficiency can lead to vast career prospects, as the programming language is applied across diverse industries and applications. Some of the careers where Python skills are in demand include:

- Web developer: Python is used to create web applications, and web development is a growing field.
- Data analyst: Python is used in data analysis and visualization, and data analytics is a growing field.
- Scientific researcher: Python is used in scientific computing applications, such as in the fields of physics, biology, and chemistry.
- Machine learning engineer: Python is widely utilized in machine learning and artificial intelligence applications.
- Software developer: Python is a versatile language that can be applied to diverse applications, making it a valuable skill for software developers

Installing Python

Once you have decided on the version of Python you want to install, the next step is to download the installation package from the official Python website. The download process may differ slightly depending on your operating system. Here are the installation instructions for Windows, macOS, and Linux:

Windows:

1. Visit the official Python website and download the latest version of Python intended for Windows operating system.
2. Once the download is complete, execute the installation file and adhere to the prompts provided to install Python.
3. Choose the destination directory where Python will be installed.
4. Choose whether to add Python to the PATH environment variable.
5. Choose whether to install additional features such as pip, tcl/tk support, and documentation.
6. Click on "Install" and after that wait for the installation process to complete.

macOS:

1. Visit the official Python website and download the latest version of Python compatible with the macOS operating system.
2. After the download is complete, run the installation file and follow the prompts provided to install Python.
3. Choose the destination directory where Python will be installed.
4. Choose whether to add Python to the PATH environment variable.
5. Choose whether to install additional features such as pip, tcl/tk support, and documentation.
6. Click "Install" and wait for the installation process to complete.

Linux:

Depending on your Linux distribution, you can either use the package manager or download the installation package from the Python website.

For example, if you are using Ubuntu, you can use the following command to install Python 3:

sudo apt-get update sudo apt-get install python3

Once Python is installed, you can check the version by running the following command in the terminal:

```
python3 --version
```

Configuring the Python Environment:

After you install Python, you may want to set up your environment by setting up variables, installing more packages, and changing your editor or integrated development environment (IDE). Here are some tips on configuring your Python environment:

Setting up environment variables:

- PATH: Add the directory where the Python executable is to the PATH variable so that you can run Python from any directory in the terminal.
- PYTHONPATH: Add the directories that hold your Python modules to the PYTHONPATH variable so that you can use them in your Python scripts.

Installing additional packages

Python's PIP serves as the package manager that facilitates effortless installation and management of Python packages.

In contrast, virtualenv is a useful tool that establishes secluded Python environments for your projects, enabling the installation of packages without impacting the global Python installation.

Customizing your editor or IDE:

There are many popular Python editors and IDEs, such as PyCharm, Visual Studio Code, Sublime Text, and Jupyter Notebook.

You can change your editor or integrated development environment (IDE) by adding plugins, changing the theme, and setting up code snippets and templates.

Overall, installing and configuring Python can seem daunting at first, but with these simple instructions and tips, you should be able to get up and running in no time.

Python Development Environments

Python development environments (IDEs) are software tools that let you create and manage Python projects in an integrated development environment. IDEs usually have features like syntax highlighting, code completion, tools for debugging, and version control built in. There are many popular Python integrated development environments (IDEs) and text editors, and each has its own pros and cons. Some of the most popular options include:

- PyCharm: JetBrains created PyCharm, a powerful IDE. It offers advanced features such as intelligent code completion, debugging tools, and integration with Git, Mercurial, and other version control systems. PyCharm also includes support for web development with Django and Flask.
- Microsoft's Visual Studio Code: It is a widely known text editor called Visual Studio Code. It features built-in support for Python, including code completion, syntax highlighting, and debugging tools. Additionally, Visual Studio Code offers support for various other languages and frameworks, making it a versatile choice for developers.

- Spyder: Spyder is an open-source Integrated Development Environment (IDE) specially created for scientific computing and data analysis. It provides a range of scientific tools and libraries, including NumPy, SciPy, and Matplotlib, as well as features such as debugging, profiling, and testing.
- Jupyter Notebook: Jupyter Notebook is a web-based tool that lets users create and share documents with live code, visualizations, and narrative text. It is commonly used in scientific computing and machine learning.
- IDLE: IDLE is the default Integrated Development Environment (IDE) that comes with standard Python distribution. It offers fundamental features like debugging tools and syntax highlighting, making it a suitable choice for beginners.

Choosing the Right IDE for Your Needs

When picking an integrated development environment (IDE) for Python development, it's important to think about your own needs and preferences. Some IDEs are designed for specific types of projects, such as scientific computing or web development, while others are more general-purpose. It's worth noting that various IDEs have distinct features and capabilities. Therefore, it is critical to select one that suits your specific needs and requirements.

Some factors to consider when choosing an IDE include:

- Features: Consider the features that are important to you, such as debugging tools, code completion, and version control integration.
- Ease of use: Choose an IDE that is easy to use and navigate, especially if you are a beginner.
- Compatibility: Make sure the IDE you choose is compatible with your operating system and other tools you may be using.

- Cost: Some IDEs, such as PyCharm, require a license for full functionality, while others are free and open source.

In conclusion, identifying the most suitable IDE is subjective and reliant on individual requirements and preferences. It is advisable to experiment with different options to discover the best fit for your programming needs.

In this chapter, we've introduced the basics of Python programming and discussed why it's such a popular and powerful language. We've also given you instructions on how to install Python and set up your development environment. We've talked about some popular Python integrated development environments (IDEs) and text editors, and we've given you tips on how to choose the right IDE for your needs. In the next chapters, we'll go into more detail about variables, data types, and control structures, which are all important parts of Python programming.

BOOK 1

The Basics of Python Programming

James P. Meyers

Chapter 1: Basic Concepts

In this chapter, we'll look at the basics of programming with Python in more depth. We will start by discussing the various data types available in Python and then move on to variables, operators, basic data structures, and control flow.

Data Types

In Python, "data types" refer to the different kinds of data that can be stored and changed. Understanding the different data types is essential, as it allows you to use the correct data type for the task at hand. The various data types in Python include:

- Numbers: These are numeric data types that can be either integers or floating-point values. Integers are whole numbers, while floating-point values are decimal numbers.
- Strings: These are a sequence of characters enclosed within single, double, or triple quotes. They are commonly used to store text.
- Booleans: These data types represent truth values and can be either True or False.

- None: This data type is used to represent the absence of a value.
- Type conversion: Type conversion refers to the process of changing one data type to another. Python provides built-in functions that allow you to convert between data types.

Data types define what kind of data can be stored and manipulated in a programming language. Since Python is dynamically typed, the interpreter automatically assigns a data type when you assign a value to a variable. This provides flexibility but can also introduce subtle bugs if you are not aware of data types.

Numeric Types

Python supports various numeric data types to store numbers, including:

Integers

- Integers (int) are whole numbers like 3, -50, 100 that have no decimal part.
- Common usage: Counting discrete quantities, indexing sequences

```
python
 code
num = 10 #integer
print(type(num)) #prints "<class 'int'>"
```

Floats

- Floats (float) represent real numbers with fractions represented after a decimal point like 2.5, -9.81, 3.141592.
- Stored in 64 bits with approx 15 decimal digits of precision.

```
python
 code
num = 2.5 #float
```

```
print(type(num)) #prints "<class 'float'>"
```

Complex Numbers

- Complex numbers (complex) are written as a + bj where a, b are floats and j represents sqrt(-1)
- Used in some math/scientific domains but less common in general programming.

```
python
 code
num = 2 + 3j
print(type(num)) #prints "<class 'complex'>
```

Exercise 1.1.1

1. Try creating variables assigned to integer, float and complex number values and printing their types to see the different numeric data types in action.
2. Also experiment with arithmetic operations between different numeric types, such as multiplying an integer with a float, and observe the result.

Boolean Type

The Boolean data type (bool) represents logical or truth values that can be either True or False. Useful for conditional testing and logic.

```
python
 code
flag = True
is_published = False
print(type(flag)) #prints "<class 'bool'>"
```

Booleans are very useful for conditional testing, which we will cover more later.

Exercise 1.1.2

1. Try assigning variables to True and False values and printing them out, to experience booleans firsthand.
2. Also build some simple logical conditions using comparison operators (like equals, not equals) together with boolean variables to get a feel for how they work.

1.1.3 Strings

Strings represent sequences of textual characters like words, phrases, sentences. Multiple ways to define:

```
python
 code
text = "Hello world"
text = 'Hello world'
long_text = """This is a long
multi-line string"""

print(type(text)) #prints "<class 'str'>"
```

- Useful string methods: upper(), lower(), replace(), split() etc.

```
python
 code
print(text.upper()) #HELLO WORLD
words = text.split(" ") #divides into words
```

String formatting

- Use f-string or str.format() to interpolate/format strings with variables

```
python
 code
```

```
name = "John"
print(f"Hello {name}!")

num = 3
print("I have {} apples".format(num))
```

Escape sequences

- Special chars like \n (newline), \t (tab) are interpreted as intended with escape seqs

```
python
 code
print("This is a \nmultiline string")
print("Language name:\tPython")
```

Exercise 1.1.3

1. Try out creating, printing and manipulating strings using different methods like upper(), lower(), title() etc to get comfortable with string handling.
2. Also experiment with string formats using f-strings and str.format(). Observe their output.
3. Finally, try using the split() method on strings to divide them into list of words.

Dynamic Typing

- Python uses dynamic typing - you can reassign variables to different data types freely

```
python
 code
x = 5 #x is integer
x = "Change value" #x is now string
```

```
print(type(x)) #Prints <class 'str'>
```

- Flexibility but can lead to bugs if types are mixed improperly

Exercise 1.1.4

1. Try declaring a variable x assigned to an integer, and reassign it to a string, list, float etc and print the types after each assigment to experience dynamic typing firsthand.

2. Also try combining variables of different types using operations like add and observe errors that occur to see issues with dynamic types.

Variables

Variables serve as containers that store data for future reference within a program. They function as a pointer to the memory location where the data is saved. When naming variables, it is crucial to adhere to naming conventions and coding best practices to ensure that your code is legible and straightforward to maintain.

- Naming conventions and best practices: Variable names should be descriptive and follow the PEP-8 style guide for Python code. Variables should also be written in lowercase, and if multiple words are used, they should be separated by an underscore.

- Variable assignment and reassignment: In Python, assigning a value to a variable can be achieved using the equal sign (=). Furthermore, it is possible to reassign a new value to the same variable.

- Augmented assignment: Augmented assignment is a shorthand method of performing arithmetic operations on a variable. It combines an arithmetic operator with the equal sign (=).

Variables are named containers used to store data values in memory during program execution. This allows you to label data and refer to it by a memorable name.

Let's learn about Python variable declaration and usage:

Assignment

- Use single = sign to assign RHS value to LHS variable
- Afterwards, variable name can be used instead of value

```
python
 code
count = 10 #Assign 10 to count
print(count) #Prints 10
```

- Can chain assignments

```
python
 code
x = y = z = 1 #x = 1, y =1, z = 1
```

Naming rules

- Variable names can contain letters, digits and underscores
- Must start with a letter or underscore
- Case sensitive (age, Age and AGE are different variables)

Valid names:

```
python
 code
age = 5
test_var = 10
currentUser = "John"
```

Invalid names:

```
python
 code
2x = 2 #Cannot start with digit
```

```
class = 5 #Cannot use keywords/reserved words
```

Dynamic typing

Variables don't declare types, and you can even change type after declaring

```
python
 code
x = 5 #x is integer
print(x, "is", type(x))

x = "Change type" #x is now string
print(x, "is", type(x))
Output:
 code
5 is <class 'int'>
Change type is <class 'str'>
```

Exercise 1.2.3

1. Try declaring variables with different assignment chains and print their values to see how chained assignments work.
2. Declare variables using the naming rules, with valid and invalid names for practice.
3. Also assign different types like strings, booleans etc to the same variable and observe typed changes.

Operators

Operators play a crucial role in performing various operations on data in Python. The language supports different types of operators, including:

- Arithmetic operators: These operators execute arithmetic operations such as addition, subtraction, multiplication, and division on numerical values.
- Comparison operators: Comparison operators are utilized to compare two values and return a Boolean value based on whether the comparison is true or false.
- Logical operators: Logical operators are employed to combine two or more conditional statements and generate a Boolean value based on the logical relationship between them.
- Bitwise operators: Bitwise operators are applied to perform bitwise operations on binary numbers.
- Identity operators: Identity operators are utilized to compare the identities of two objects and return a Boolean value based on whether they have the same identity or not.
- Membership operators: Membership operators are applied to check if a value is present in a sequence and return a Boolean value based on whether the value is present in the sequence or not.

Operators are symbols that carry out operations on operands (variables, values). Python supports various types:

Arithmetic Operators

Used to perform numeric calculations

Operator	**Description**	**Example**
+	Addition	x + y
-	Subtraction	x - y
*	Multiplication	x * y
/	Float division	x / y
//	Integer division	x // y
%	Modulo (remainder)	x % y
**	Exponent	x ** y

```
python
 code
a = 30
b = 20
print(a + b) #50
print(a - b) #10

x = 2
print(x ** 3) #8 (2 * 2 * 2)
```

Exercise 1.3.1

1. Try out examples of using different arithmetic operators on numeric operands to get familiar with them.
2. Experiment with integer vs float division using the / and // operators to see the difference in behavior.
3. Use the % modulo operator applied to integers and observe the remainder result.

Comparison Operators

Allow comparing two values, returns bool result. Used widely in conditional testing.

Operator	**Description**	**Example**
==	Equals	x == y
!=	Not equals	x != y
>	Greater than	x > y
<	Less than	x < y
>=	Greater than or equals	x >= y
<=	Less than or equals	x <= y

```
python
 code
num1 = 10
num2 = 20

print(num1 > num2) #False
print(num1 != num2) #True
print(num1 <= num2) #True
```

Logical Operators

- Apply logical conditions between bool operands/expressions. Return bool.

Operator	Description	Example
and	Returns True if both operands True	x and y
or	Returns True if either operand True	x or y
not	Inverts True/False value	not x

```
python
 code
x = True
y = False
print(x and y) #False - both aren't True
print(x or y) #True - x is True
print(not x) #Negates to False
```

Bitwise Operators

Lower-level operators that work on bits of integers. Some examples:

```
python
 code
a = 60            # 0011 1100
```

```
b = 13                # 0000 1101

print(a & b)          # 0000 1100 = 12
print(a | b)          # 0011 1101 = 61
print(a ^ b)          # 0011 0001 = 49
print(~a )            # 1100 0011 = -61
print(a << 2)         # 1111 0000 = 240
print(a >> 2)         # 0000 1111 = 15
```

Exercise 1.3.2 - 1.3.4

1. Experiment with comparison operators using different integer, float and string variables to observe boolean outcomes.

2. Try building compound logical boolean expressions with AND/OR/NOT operators.

3. Look up Bitwise operators documentation and test out their functionality on sample integer values to learn.

Basic Data Structures

Data structures in Python refer to the different ways of storing and organizing data. Python provides four built-in data structures: lists, tuples, sets, and dictionaries.

- Lists: Lists store a collection of values and are mutable, implying that their contents can be changed.

- Tuples: Tuples are similar to lists but are immutable, indicating that their contents cannot be modified.

- Sets: Sets hold a collection of unique values, and they are mutable and unordered.

- Dictionaries: Dictionaries store key-value pairs and are mutable and unordered.

Beyond individual values, Python provides built-in data structure types to organize multiple related values together:

Lists

Stores ordered, indexed collections of items allowing duplicate values.

Creating lists:

```
python
 code
nums = [1, 2, 3] #Square brackets
multi_type = ["Hi", 5, True] #Multi-typed
matrix = [[1,2,3], [4,5,6]] #Multidimensional
```

Accessing elements:

```
python
 code
print(nums[0]) #Prints first element
print(matrix[1][2]) #Prints 6
```

Modifying:

```
python
 code
nums[1] = 20 #Assign new value
nums.append(30) #Add value to end
nums.insert(1, 25) #Insert value at index
```

Tuples

Like lists but elements cannot be changed after creation (immutable). Defined using () parenthesis instead of [].

Creating tuples:

```python
code
point = (1, 2)
book = ("Python 101", 2020, 4.5)
```

Trying to modify raises error:

```python
code
point[0] = 2 #Gives error
```

Dictionaries

Stores mappings of unique keys to values, similar to map/hash table. Keys must be immutable types.

Creating dictionaries:

```python
code
user = {"name": "John", "id": 1, "verified": True}
products = {} #Empty dict
```

Access & modify:

```python
code
print(user["name"]) # Get value of "name" key

user["id"] = 2 # Update value of "id"
print(user) # Prints {'name': 'John', 'id': 2,
'verified': True}
```

Exercise 1.4.1 - 1.4.3

1. Practice creating different lists, tuples and dictionaries, accessing and printing their values.

2. Try modifying lists by adding, changing and removing elements with different methods. Observe errors with tuples.

3. Create a custom dictionary mapping product names to prices. Practice accessing, updating and adding key-value pairs.

Control Flow

Control flow pertains to the sequence of execution of statements in a program. Python incorporates various control flow statements, including:

- with if/else: Conditional statements are utilized to execute different blocks of code depending on whether a condition is true or false.

- Loops with for and while: Loops are utilized to execute a block of code repeatedly. Python offers two types of loops: for loops and while loops.

for Loops

The for loop iterates over items of a sequence and runs a code block once for each item.Sequences like strings, lists, tuples can be used with for.

Syntax:

```
 code
for item in sequence:
   #code block
```

Example:

```
python
 code
fruits = ["apple", "banana", "mango"]
for fruit in fruits:
   print("I have an", fruit)
Output:
```

```
code
I have an apple
I have an banana
I have an mango
```

- The loop variable fruit takes the value of next sequence item in each iteration
- Code under loop runs 3 times, once for each item

You can also directly iterate tuples, dictionaries and other sequences besides lists:

```
python
 code
person = ("John", 30, "New York")
for value in person:
   print(value) #Prints items
```

range()

To iterate a fixed number of times instead of over a sequence, use the range() type.

Syntax:

```
 code
for i in range(start, stop, step_size):
   #code block
```

Example: Print numbers from 1 to 10

```
python
 code
for i in range(1, 11):
   print(i)
Output:
 code
```

```
1
2
3
...
10
```

- start: Starting number (default 0)
- stop: Generate numbers up to, but not including this number
- step_size: Difference between numbers (default 1)

Exercise 1.1.1.1:

1. Iterate over a list of fruits and print their names
2. Print multiples of 3 from 0 to 30 using range() and for

for/else

A little known construct - the else block after a for loop is executed after the loop ends normally. Useful to detect early termination.

```
python
 code
for i in range(3):
   print(i)
else:
   print("Loop ended")
Output:
 code
0
1
2
```

Loop ended

- else won't run if loop stops prematurely e.g using break

Exercise 1.1.1.2:

1. Break out early from a for/else loop and observe if else runs
2. Print numbers divisible by 10 from a range using for/else

while Loops

While executes a code block repeatedly as long as a condition is true.

Syntax:

```
code
while condition:
   #code block
```

Example: Print 0 to 4

```
python
code
x = 0
while x < 5:
   print(x)
   x += 1 #Increment x
Output:
code
0
1
2
3
4
```

- Condition is checked first before loop body runs
- Useful when number of iterations isn't known beforehand

Exercise 1.1.2:

1. Print squares from 1 to 10 using a while and print
2. Sum integers entered by user until 0 is entered

while/else

while also supports an optional else block that runs if loop exits normally.

```
python
 code
x = 5
while x > 0:
   print(x)
   x -= 1
else:
   print('Countdown finished')
```

- else won't execute if while loop stops due to break

Exercise 1.1.2.1:

1. Break early from a while loop to skip else execution
2. Print numbers from 5 down to 1 using while/else

Nested Loops

You can have loops inside other loops to create nested/multi-level iterations.

Syntax:

```
python
 code
for i in range(5):
   for j in range(3):
     print(i, j)
```

```
Output:
 code
0 0
0 1
0 2
1 0
...
```

- Inner loop runs completely before going to next iteration of outer loop

Very useful for mulit-dimensional iteration like 2D lists:

```
python
 code
matrix = [[1,2], [3,4]]

for row in matrix:
   for col in row:
      print(col)
```

Exercise 1.1.3:

1. Print multiplication tables from 2 to 5 using nested loops
2. Iterate a 2D list and print coordinates

Loop Control Statements

Some statements like break, continue pass allow you to control loop execution flow.

break

Terminates and exits the closest enclosing loop.

Example: Exit after 3 iterations

python

code

```
for i in range(10):
    if i > 2:
        break
    print(i)
```

Output:

code

```
0
1
2
```

- After break hits, directly jumps to the code after loop

continue

Jumps to the next iteration, skipping the code after it for current loop.

python

code

```
for i in range(6):
    if i % 2 != 0: #Not evenly divisible by 2
        continue
    print(i)
```

Output:

code

```
0
2
4
```

- Skips odd numbers, only prints even values

pass

A null statement that instructs interpreter to do nothing. Used as placeholder when syntax requires a statement.

```
python
 code
if test == False:
  pass #Do nothing
```

Exercise 1.2.1 - 1.2.3:

1. Break early from a fruit printing loop if 'banana' is encountered
2. Continue to next iteration in a loop if number is divisible by 7
3. Use pass as placeholder for future logic in loops/conditionals

Python Conditional Statements

Python provides three main conditional statements to control the flow of execution - if, else and elif statements. These allow checking conditions and executing different blocks of code based on whether the conditions evaluate to True or False. Conditional statements are extremely useful in writing Python programs that can make smart decisions. Let's learn about each of these in detail:

If Statement

The if statement is used to check a condition and execute a block of code if the condition evaluates to True. The basic syntax is:

```
python
 code
if condition:
    # lines of code to execute if condition is True
```

Here, the condition after the if statement is checked first. If it is True, then the indented lines of code inside the if block will execute. If the condition is False, then the code inside the if block is skipped.

For example:

```
python
 code
num = 15
if num > 10:
    print("Num is greater than 10")
```

Here, the condition num > 10 evaluates to True as num is 15. So the print statement inside the if block will execute and "Num is greater than 10" will be printed.

The condition in an if statement can use any conditional expressions like equality checks (==), comparisons (<, > etc), membership operators (in) etc to evaluate to True or False.

If-Else Statement

The if-else statement allows executing one block of code if the condition is True and another block of code if the condition is False. The syntax is:

```
python
 code
if condition:
    # lines to execute if condition True
else:
    # lines to execute if condition False
```

For example:

```
python
 code
```

```
num = 7
if num > 10:
    print("Num is greater than 10")
```

else:

```
    print("Num is less than 10")
```

Here, the else part will execute since num > 10 evaluates to False for num = 7. So this prints "Num is less than 10".

The else block allows covering both cases with if and else blocks - when the condition is True or False.

Elif Statement

The elif statement allows chaining multiple conditions to check and executing different code blocks based on the first condition that evaluates to True. For example:

```
python
 code
num = 15
if num > 20:
   print("Num is greater than 20")
elif num > 10:
   print("Num is greater than 10")
elif num > 5:
   print("Num is greater than 5")
else:
   print("Num is less than 5")
```

Here, first num > 20 is checked and is False. Next, num > 10 is True. So the block under this elif will execute printing "Num is greater than 10". Using a series of elif allows checking multiple conditions easily in Python.

An if-elif-else chain allows only one block of code to execute as the conditions are checked in order and the block under first True condition executes. Rest of the chain is skipped.

Nested If Statement

Conditional statements can also be nested to check complex conditions with multiple decisions possible. Nested if statements have an if condition inside another if or else block.

For example:

```
python
 code
num = 14
if num >= 10:
    print("Num is greater than 10")
    if num == 14:
        print("Specifically num is 14")
```

First the outer check num >=10 is done which is True here. So the nested if block is reached and here num == 14 so again prints "Specifically num is 14".

Nesting conditional statements controls execution flow across multiple checks and conditional codes.

One Line Conditional Statements

Small conditional checks can also be written in a single line for brevity using ternary operators and lambdas as given below:

```
python
 code
value = 10 if num > 5 else 0  # Ternary operator
is_positive = (lambda num: True if num > 0 else
```

```
False)(value) # Lambda function
```

Here for the ternary operator, if num > 5 evaluates to True, value is set to 10, else it is set to 0. Similarly, the lambda function checks if value is > 0 and returns True/False.

Multiple Conditions in If Statement

An if statement can also check multiple conditions using logical operators like and, or. For example:

```
python
 code
num = 15
if num >= 10 and num <= 20:
    print("Between 10 and 20")
```

This checks two conditions joined with a logical and operator. Both conditions need to evaluate to True for the overall condition to be True and the code inside the if to execute.

Similarly, or can be used to check if any one of multiple conditions is True. Multiple complex conditions can be built using logical operators in this way.

Exercises

1. Write an if-else statement that prints "Num is odd" if the num variable holds an odd number and "Num is even" if it holds an even number
2. Write an if-elif-else chain that prints "Positive" if num > 0, "Negative" if num < 0 and "Zero" if num = 0
3. Write nested if statements for the following logic - if age > 60, print "Senior Citizen". If age is also >= 65, print "Additional benefits eligible"

4. Convert the nested if statements in Q3 to use only if-elif-else statements
5. Write a one line conditional statement using lambda to check if num is divisible by 5
6. Write an if statement that prints "Valid" if var starts with A or B or C and is 10 to 20 characters long else prints "Invalid"

Functions and Modules

Functions and Parameters

As a Python programmer, you'll find yourself using functions frequently. A function is a reusable block of code that performs a specific task. You can define a function to perform a task once and then call it multiple times throughout your code. This approach is more efficient and less prone to errors than writing the same code repeatedly.

Defining and Calling Functions

In Python, the syntax for defining a function involves utilizing the def keyword, followed by the function name and parentheses.

Inside the parentheses, you can define any parameters the function needs to take in. Then, you use a colon to start the function's code block. Here's an example of a simple function:

```
def greet(name):
    print(f"Hello, {name}!")
```

This function takes in a single parameter called name and prints a greeting message using that name. To call this function, you simply write the function name followed by the parameter value in parentheses:

```
greet("Alice")
```

This code would output "Hello, Alice!" to the console.

Positional and Keyword Arguments

Functions can take in parameters in two ways: positional and keyword arguments. Positional arguments are passed in order, while keyword arguments are passed using the argument name. Here's an example:

```
def describe_pet(name, animal_type):
    print(f"My {animal_type}'s name is {name}.")
describe_pet("Buddy", "dog")
describe_pet(animal_type="cat", name="Whiskers")
```

In the first call to describe_pet, "Buddy" is passed as the first argument (name) and "dog" as the second argument (animal_type). In the second call, the order is reversed, but the argument names are explicitly stated. Both calls to the function will output "My dog's name is Buddy."

User Defined vs Built in Functions

User Defined Functions

User-defined functions are created by the programmer to execute sections of code upon being called or invoked. They allow for reusable pieces of logic written once to be utilized wherever needed. Functions also enable abstraction in Python code.

Here is the general syntax for defining a function in Python:

```
python
 code
def function_name(parameters):
   statements
   return value
```

Let's see an example function definition that takes in two integer inputs, adds them together, and returns the sum:

```
python
 code
def add_nums(num1, num2):
   sum = num1 + num2
   return sum
```

The function is named add_nums and has two parameters - num1 and num2. Inside the function body, the two numbers are added and stored in sum. This sum is returned as the output.

To call this function from somewhere else in the code:

```
python
 code
result = add_nums(5, 3)
print(result) # Prints 8
```

The values 5 and 3 are passed to the num1 and num2 parameters respectively when calling add_nums. The function executes its body, storing the sum 8 in the result variable which is then printed.

So in essence, user-defined functions encapsulate reusable logic to be executed on demand through function calls. They are powerful for abstraction and decomposing complex programs into simpler building blocks.

Built-In Functions

Python also comes packed with many built-in functions that are readily available to us. These execute common operations like conversion, I/O, mathematics etc. so we don't have to write our own functionality.

For example, Python has a built-in print() function that prints text to the console:

```
python
 code
print("Hello World!") # Prints Hello World!
```

Some commonly used built-in functions include:

- len() - Returns length of strings, lists etc.
- int()/float()/str() - Type conversion functions

- max()/min() - Return maximum & minimum of arguments
- round() - Rounds a floating point value
- input() - Reads user input from console

So in summary, built-in functions are pre-defined by Python itself while user-defined functions are created by the programmer. But both serve the purpose of reusable modular code.

Exercises

1. Define a function calculate_sum() that takes in a numeric list as argument and returns the sum of all numbers in that list. Call this function to find the sum of list [10, 15, 20] and print it.
2. Print the absolute value of -15 using the built-in abs() function. Also print the minimum of numbers 23, 89, 5 using the min() function.

Function Arguments

When defining a function in Python, we can specify parameters that act as variables to hold the inputs passed as arguments while calling that function. These function arguments control how input parameters are handled within the function.

There are four types of function arguments in Python:

1. Default Arguments
2. Required Arguments
3. Keyword Arguments
4. Variable-length Arguments

Let's explore them in detail with examples:

Default Arguments

Default arguments allow a default value to be used for a parameter if no argument is passed for it. This makes invoking functions easier when some parameters are optionally specified.

Here is a function definition using default arguments:

```
python
 code
def full_name(first_name, last_name, middle_name=""):
    name = first_name + " " + middle_name + " " +
last_name
    return name
```

Here the middle_name parameter has a default empty string value specified. So we can call the function with or without passing the middle name -

```
python
 code
print(full_name("John", "Doe")) # John Doe
print(full_name("Sara", "Williams", "Marie")) # Sara
Marie Williams
```

As we can see, default arguments increase flexibility while calling functions in Python.

Required Arguments

Required arguments, as the name suggests, are parameters that must be passed values for while calling the function. Not passing these required arguments will result in errors.

Here is how we define and call functions using required arguments:

```
python
 code
def power(base, exponent):
   result = base**exponent
```

```
   print(f"{base} raised to power {exponent} is
{result}")

power(2, 3) # Works fine

power(2) # Error - missing required argument exponent
```

So for required parameters, values must be passed while invocation otherwise errors occur.

Keyword Arguments

Keyword arguments allow function parameters to be passed values by name at call time specifically. This provides more readability with argument order independence.

For example:

```
python
 code
def student_details(name, age, class_level):
   print(name, age, class_level)

student_details("Jim", 16, 10)

student_details(name = "Jim", age = 16, class_level =
10)
```

Here there is no difference between the function calls. But with keyword args, if we only wanted to pass the name leaving other params as defaults:

```
python
 code
student_details(name="Jim")
```

This enhances readability by not needing to worry about argument order. Keyword args also allow selective param passing.

Variable-length Arguments

Variable-length args allow arbitrary number of arguments to be directly passed grouped together at call time. Common ones are -

- *args - Accepts variable number of non-keyword arguments
- **kwargs - Accepts variable number of keyword arguments

Usage example:

```
python
 code
def total_sums(*args):
   sum = 0
   for num in args:
     sum += num
   return sum
print(total_sums(1, 5, 8)) # 14 - Accepts variable
non-keyword args
```

The *args take in as many numeric arguments as provided. Similarly, we can use **kwargs to get a dict of keyword arguments -

```
python
 code
def user_details(**kwargs):
   for key, value in kwargs.items():
     print(f"{key}: {value}")

user_details(name="Lisa", age=25, gender="Female")
# Prints:
# name: Lisa
# age: 25
# gender: Female
```

So in essence, variable-length arguments provide flexibility to pass arbitrary number of arguments to functions in Python.

Exercises

1. Define a function exponent() to calculate the exponent of a number using default, required and keyword arguments. Call it to find 2^4 and 3^3.
2. Define a sum_all() function using *args to find the sum of a variable number of integers passed to it.

Docstrings

In Python, documentation strings or docstrings allow functions, modules, classes etc. to have associated metadata descriptions. These provide crucial insight into component purpose, usage, parameters, outputs etc. directly in the source code itself.

- Here is how to define docstrings:

```
python
 code
def print_line():
   """This function prints a horizontal line"""
   print("--------------------------")

print(print_line.__doc__) # Access docstring
# Prints: This function prints a horizontal line
```

The docstring comes right after the function header under the declaration. Using a triple quotes syntax, we describe what the function does.

We can access the docstring programatically like shown above with the __doc__ special attribute. This allows inspection about metadata like intended usage.

Some key docstring conventions to follow:

- Always use triple double or single quotes
- First line should be a short concise summary
- Elaborate further with long description if needed
- Specify function arguments, return values, exceptions if applicable
- Limit line width to 72 characters for readability

Here is an example of a detailed docstring:

```
python
 code
def calculate_mean(num_list):
    """Calculates average mean of numbers in a given
list.

    Args:
        num_list (list of ints/floats): The list of
numbers to calculate mean for

    Returns:
        float: The calculated average mean
    """
    mean = sum(num_list) / len(num_list)
    return mean
```

Following conventions and best practices for docstrings enhances understandability and usability of code components in Python by documenting functionality and usage right alongside implementation.

Exercises

1. Define a function to find the maximum of three numbers. Write a proper docstring for it specifying what it does, parameters, and return value.

2. Access and print docstring of Python's built-in print() and len() functions.

Return Statement

The return statement in Python explicitly returns a value from a function back to the caller code. This enables assigning function execution results to variables for further processing.

Here is a simple example:

```
python
 code
def add_nums(num1, num2):
   sum = num1 + num2
   return sum

result = add_nums(5, 3)
print(result) # 8
```

When return sum executes inside add_nums, value of sum is sent back. This output 8 is assigned to result variable and printed.

Some key points on return statement:

- A function terminates execution immediately after return stmt
- Values following return like further statements won't execute
- Returns None if no value is explicitly specified
- Can return any data type - arrays, objects etc.

- Can return multiple values as tuple

Let's see some examples to understand these better:

Terminates function execution

```
python
 code
def add_sub(num1, num2):
    sum = num1 + num2
    return sum
    print("This won't print after return above")

print(add_sub(5, 3)) # 8
```

Here after return executes, further print statement doesn't run.

Returns None if no return value:

```
python
 code
def print_name(name):
   print(name)

print(print_name("John")) # None
```

Since no return stmt, print_name returns None implicitly.

Returns multiple values (as tuple):

```
python
 code
def min_max(nums):
   min = min(nums)
   max = max(nums)
   return min, max
```

```
min, max = min_max([5, 2, 7, 3])
print(min) # 2
print(max) # 7
```

So in summary, return statement returns execution control back to caller code while also sending function outputs. Properly using returns is vital for reusable modular functions.

Exercises

1. Define a currency converter function from USD to EUR. Use return statement properly and call this function to get the converted EUR value for 10 USD.
2. Define a function to return multiple values (name, age) for a user passed. Call it for name="Sam" and age=25.

Returning Values

Functions don't have to just perform tasks; they can also return values. To return a value from a function, you use the return keyword followed by the value you want to return. Here's an example:

```
def square(x):
    return x ** 2
result = square(5)
print(result)  # outputs 25
```

This function takes in a parameter x and returns its square. The value returned by the function is assigned to the variable result, which is then printed to the console.

Multiple Return Values

Functions can also return multiple values. To do this, you simply separate the values you want to return with commas. Here's an example:

```
def divide(x, y):
    quotient = x // y
    remainder = x % y
    return quotient, remainder
result1, result2 = divide(10, 3)
print(result1)  # outputs 3
print(result2)  # outputs 1
```

This function takes in two parameters x and y and returns their quotient and remainder. The values returned by the function are assigned to two variables result1 and result2, which are then printed to the console.

Built-in Functions

Python comes with a wide range of built-in functions that you can use in your code. These functions are always available, so you don't have to define them yourself. Here's an overview of some commonly used built-in functions:

- print(): Prints text to the console.
- input(): Reads input from the user.
- len(): Returns the length of an iterable, such as a string or list.
- range(): Generates a sequence of numbers.
- sum(): Returns the sum of a list of numbers.
- max(): Returns the maximum value in a list of numbers.
- min(): Returns the minimum value in a list of numbers.
- str(): Converts an object to a string.
- int(): Converts a string or float to an integer.
- float(): Converts a string or integer to a float.

- bool(): Converts a value to a Boolean (True or False).
- type(): Returns the type of an object.
- help(): Displays documentation for an object.

These functions are just a small sample of what's available. You can find a full list of Python's built-in functions in the Python documentation.

Importing Modules

While Python's built-in functions are useful, there will be times when you need to use additional functionality that's not included in the standard library. That's where modules come in. A module is a file containing Python code that defines functions, classes, and other objects. By importing a module, you can use its functionality in your code.

Overview of Python Modules

A wide range of third-party modules are accessible for Python, spanning from scientific computing to web development. Notably, some well-known modules comprise:

- Numpy: Offers support for multi-dimensional arrays and matrices, particularly large ones.
- Pandas: Provides data analysis tools.
- Matplotlib: Provides data visualization tools.
- Django: A popular web framework.
- Requests: Provides tools for making HTTP requests.

There are many more modules available, and you can even create your own. In the next section, we'll look at how to import and use modules in your code.

Importing Modules in Your Code

To include a module in your Python program, you use the import statement followed by the name of the module. For instance:

```
import math
result = math.sqrt(25)
print(result) # outputs 5.0
```

The aforementioned code includes the math module, which offers a variety of mathematical functions. Then, the sqrt() function is utilized on the imported math module to calculate the square root of 25, after which the outcome is printed to the console.

Furthermore, you can import specific functions or classes from a module utilizing the from keyword. Here's an example:

```
from random import randint
result = randint(1, 10)
print(result) # outputs a random integer between 1
and 10
```

This code imports the randint() function from the random module, which generates a random integer between two specified values. The randint() function is then called directly, without utilizing the random module name.

Creating and Using Your Own Modules

In addition to using third-party modules, you can also create your own modules. To do this, you simply create a new Python file containing your module code, and then import it into your main code as we saw in the previous section.

Creating a Custom Python Module

Here's an example of a simple custom module that defines a function for calculating the area of a circle:

```
# circle.py
import math
def area(radius):
    return math.pi * radius ** 2
```

This code defines a single function area() that takes in a radius parameter and returns the area of a circle with that radius. Note that the math module is imported to access the value of pi.

Using a Custom Python Module

To use the circle module in your main code, you simply import it as we saw in the previous section:

```
import circle
result = circle.area(5)
print(result)  # outputs 78.53981633974483
```

This code imports the circle module and calls its area() function with a radius of 5. The result is printed to the console.

Organizing Your Code with Modules

As your codebase grows, it can become difficult to manage all of your functions and classes in a single file. That's where modules come in handy - they allow you to organize your code into separate files that can be imported and used in other parts of your code.

A common approach is to create a separate module file for each logical unit of your code. For example, you might create a module for handling database connections, another module for handling user authentication, and so on. This makes it easier to locate and update specific parts of your codebase.

You can also use sub-packages to further organize your code. A sub-package is simply a directory containing one or more module files. For example, you might create a sub-package called models that contains modules for defining your data models.

To import a module from a sub-package, you use dot notation. For example, to import a module called user from a sub-package called models, you would use the following code:

```
from myapp.models import user
```

This code imports the user module from the models sub-package in a project called myapp.

Functions and modules are essential tools for writing organized, maintainable Python code. Functions allow you to encapsulate reusable blocks of code, while modules allow you to organize your code into separate files and re-use code across multiple projects. By understanding how to define and call functions, return values, use built-in functions, and import and create custom modules, you can take your Python programming skills to the next level.

Practical Exercise: Building a Simple Calculator

In this exercise, you will build a simple calculator script that leverages what you've learned about functions and function arguments to handle basic numeric operations.

1. First, import the math package which contains built-in math functions

```
python
 code
import math
```

2. Define four functions for add(), subtract(), multiply(), divide(). Each should take two numbers as arguments and return the computed result.

3. Create a main() function that prints a menu, takes user's operation choice and calls the appropriate function to compute entered numbers.

4. Call the main() function to run the calculator. Use return statements properly to work with outputs within this structure.

This is a great way to bring together all function concepts covered so far to build something practical and usable.

Practical Exercise: Creating and Manipulating Data Structures

Practice your skills at creating and manipulating data collections using built-in Python data structures and custom functions:

1. Define a custom function create_user() that accepts name, age and country to return a dictionary with those keys

2. Append 5 created user dictionaries to an initially empty users list by calling your create_user()

3. Define two functions - count_users_by_country() and get_max_age() that accept the users list as argument for analysis

4. Call your data analysis functions on the user's list to see Python's abilities at manipulating data

This provides a practical usage demo for both built-in and user-defined functions to manage collections of structured data.

These are two great hands-on exercises to supplement the chapter's overall learnings. You can build several such creative exercises to apply core concepts.

Chapter 2: Input and Output

Input and output (I/O) is a fundamental concept in programming, as it allows you to interact with users, read and write data to files, and handle errors that may occur during the execution of your code. In this chapter, we'll explore the various ways you can perform I/O in Python, including standard input/output, reading and writing files, and error handling.

Standard Input/Output

Python provides a simple and intuitive way to read and write data to and from the console. This is known as standard input/output (or simply, stdin/stdout), and is achieved using the input() and print() functions.

Basic input/output with Python

The input() function enables you to ask the user for input from the console. The code below, for instance, prompts the user to enter their name and subsequently prints a greeting using that name:

```
name = input("Enter your name: ")
print("Hello, " + name + "!")
```

On the other hand, the print() function permits you to display data to the console. By default, the print() function separates one or more arguments with spaces. The following code, for example, outputs a message to the console:

```
print("Hello, world!")
```

You can also use special characters such as \n to insert newlines, or \t to insert tabs, in your output.

Reading and writing to the console

In addition to input() and print(), Python provides two other functions for reading and writing data to and from the console: sys.stdin and sys.stdout. These are used when you need to perform more advanced I/O operations, such as reading multiple lines of input, or redirecting output to a file.

To read input from the console using sys.stdin, you can use the input() function in combination with the sys.stdin.readline() method. For example, the following code reads multiple lines of input from the console until the user types "quit":

```
import sys
while True:
    line = sys.stdin.readline().strip()
    if line == "quit":
        break
    print("You entered:", line)
```

Similarly, to write output to the console using sys.stdout, you can use the print() function in combination with the sys.stdout.write() method. For example, the following code redirects the output of print() to a file called "output.txt":

```
import sys
sys.stdout = open("output.txt", "w")
print("Hello, world!")
```

Reading and Writing Files

Reading text and binary files with Python

Reading and writing data to files is an important part of any programming language, and Python makes it easy to work with both text and binary files.

To access the contents of a text file in Python, you can utilize the open() function with the "r" mode. The function returns a file object that you can use to access the contents of the file. The code below, for instance, reads the contents of a file named "example.txt":

```
with open("example.txt", "r") as f:
    contents = f.read()
    print(contents)
```

You can also read the contents of a file line-by-line using the readline() method:

```
with open("example.txt", "r") as f:
    line = f.readline()
    while line:
        print(line)
        line = f.readline()
```

To read a binary file in Python, you can use the open() function with the "rb" mode. This returns a file object that you can use to read the contents of the file as bytes. For example, the following code reads the contents of a binary file called "example.bin":

```
with open("example.bin", "rb") as f:
    contents = f.read()
    print(contents)
```

Similarly, you can use the read() method to read a certain number of bytes from the file, or the readline() method to read a certain number of bytes up to the next newline character.

Writing data to files

To save data to a file in Python, you can use the open() function with the "w" mode. The function returns a file object that you can use to write data to the file. The code below, for instance, writes a message to a file named "output.txt":

```
with open("output.txt", "w") as f:
    f.write("Hello, world!")
```

You can also write data to a file line-by-line using the write() method:

```
with open("output.txt", "w") as f:
    f.write("Line 1\n")
    f.write("Line 2\n")
    f.write("Line 3\n")
```

When writing to a binary file, you should use the "wb" mode instead of the "w" mode.

Error Handling

Handling errors in programming is a necessary skill, and it's important to do so in a way that is efficient and effective. In Python, you can handle errors by using try/except blocks, which provide a flexible and powerful way to handle errors in your code.

Handling exceptions with try/except blocks

A try/except block allows you to try a block of code, and then catch any exceptions (i.e., errors) that occur. This allows you to handle errors in a way that makes sense for your program, without crashing the entire program.

For example, the following code attempts to open a file called "example.txt", but catches any FileNotFoundError exceptions that occur:

```
try:
    with open("example.txt", "r") as f:
        contents = f.read()
        print(contents)
except FileNotFoundError:
    print("File not found!")
```

You can also catch multiple exceptions using a single try/except block:

```
try:
    # some code here
except (Exception1, Exception2):
    # handle exception 1 or 2
except Exception3:
    # handle exception 3
```

Raising your own exceptions

Sometimes, you may want to raise your own exceptions to indicate that something unexpected has happened in your program. You can do this using the raise statement, followed by an exception object.

For example, the following code raises a ValueError exception if the user enters a negative number:

```
num = int(input("Enter a positive number: "))
if num < 0:
    raise ValueError("Number must be positive!")
```

You can also define your own custom exceptions by creating a new class that inherits from the Exception class:

```
class CustomException(Exception):
    pass
raise CustomException("Something went wrong!")
```

In this chapter, we've covered the basics of input and output in Python, including standard input/output, reading and writing files, and error handling. By mastering these concepts, you'll be able to write more robust and reliable programs that interact with users, read and write data to files, and handle errors gracefully. Keep practicing these concepts to become a skilled Python programmer.

Practical Exercise: File Manipulation and Error Handling

Applying the concepts covered in this chapter, let's build a Python script interacting with files and handling errors:

1. Import os and csv modules which provide file system and CSV parsing functionality
2. Define function read_csv() accepting a filename

- Open the file in a try/except block to catch errors
- Use csv module to read rows into a list

- Return the list

3. Define function write_file() taking name and content

- Try to open a new file to write the content
- Handle ValueError if invalid inputs
- Write provided content & return success status

4. Call read_csv() to read a sample CSV file

- Pass filename that may not exist on disk

5. Call write_file() to write content to a new text file

Some example calls would be:

```
python
 code
rows = read_csv('data.csv') # Catches filenotfound
error

status = write_file('results.txt', 'Success!') #
Writes file
```

This demonstrates real-world usage of error handling and interfacing with OS through file usage and manipulation.

The exercise covers core Python concepts like imports, exception handling, interacting with environment while also solving practical programming needs. Feel free to enhance and customize it further.

Chapter 3: Object-Oriented Programming

Object-oriented programming (OOP) is a programming approach that uses objects to store both data and the methods to manipulate that data. Python is a language that supports OOP and allows developers to create classes and objects, which are fundamental components of OOP. This chapter will cover the basics of OOP in Python and how to utilize it to write efficient and maintainable code.

Classes and Objects

In Python, a class is a plan or template for building objects. It specifies a set of characteristics and actions that the objects generated from the class will have. To generate an object from a class, you have to first define the class. Here's an example of a simple class definition in Python:

```
class Person:
def init(self, name, age):
self.name = name
self.age = age
def say_hello(self):
print(f"Hello, my name is {self.name} and I'm {self.
age} years old.")
```

In this example, we establish a class named "Person" with two attributes (name and age) and one method (say_hello). The **init** method is a unique method that is triggered when an object is generated from the class. It initializes the attributes of the object with the values passed as arguments to the constructor. The self parameter refers to the object that is being created.

To generate an object from the Person class, we can use the following code:

```
person1 = Person("Alice", 30)
```

This generates an object of the Person class with the name "Alice" and age 30. We can access the attributes and methods of the object using the dot notation:

```
print(person1.name)
print(person1.age)
person1.say_hello()
```

This will produce the following output:

```
Alice
30

Hello, my name is Alice and I'm 30 years old.
```

Methods and Attributes

In Python, methods are functions that are defined inside a class and can manipulate the attributes of the object. These attributes are variables that store the state of the object. The Person class example above has attributes of name and age. Methods are used to operate on these attributes or provide specific functionality to the object. The code provides an example of a class with two methods.

```
class Rectangle:
    def __init__(self, width, height):
        self.width = width
        self.height = height

    def area(self):
        return self.width * self.height

    def perimeter(self):
        return 2 * (self.width + self.height)
```

This particular example demonstrates the creation of a class named Rectangle which contains two attributes: width and height, as well as two methods: area and perimeter. The area method returns the calculated area of the rectangle, whereas the perimeter method returns the calculated perimeter of the rectangle. To instantiate an object of the Rectangle class, you can use the provided code:

```
rectangle1 = Rectangle(10, 20)
```

This creates an object of the Rectangle class with a width of 10 and a height of 20. We can call the methods of the object using the dot notation:

```
print(rectangle1.area())
print(rectangle1.perimeter())
```

This will output:

```
 code
200
60
```

Attributes can also be accessed and modified directly, without using a method. Here's an example:

```
class Counter:
    def __init__(self):
        self.count = 0

    def increment(self):
        self.count
```

Inheritance

In object-oriented programming, inheritance is a useful concept that enables us to form new classes by building upon existing ones. By inheriting from an existing class, we can create a new class called a child class, with the existing class becoming the parent class or superclass.

The Benefits of Inheriting Properties and Methods From Parent Classes

Inheritance enables us to utilize the properties and methods of an existing class in a new class. Whenever a child class inherits from a parent class, it gains access to all of the properties and methods of the parent class. This makes it easier to create new classes that have similar functionality to existing classes, without having to duplicate code.

To inherit from a parent class, we simply define the child class with the parent class as a parameter in the class definition. For example, to create a new class called Car that inherits from the Vehicle class, we would define it as follows:kotlin code

```
class Car(Vehicle):
    pass
```

Now, the Car class has access to all the properties and methods of the Vehicle class. We can also override the properties and methods of the parent class if we want to change their behavior in the child class.

Creating child classes

Inheritance also allows us to create more specialized classes based on existing classes. For example, we could create a Truck class that inherits from the Vehicle class but has additional properties and methods specific to trucks.

To create a child class with additional properties and methods, we simply define them in the child class. For example:

```
class Truck(Vehicle):
    def __init__(self, make, model, year, payload_
capacity):
        super().__init__(make, model, year)
        self.payload_capacity = payload_capacity

    def load_cargo(self, weight):
        if weight > self.payload_capacity:
            raise ValueError("Cargo too heavy for
truck")
        else:
            print("Loading cargo...")
```

Here, the Truck class inherits from the Vehicle class and adds a payload_capacity property and a load_cargo method.

Polymorphism

Polymorphism is another important concept in object-oriented programming. It allows us to use the same interface to represent different types of objects. This means that we can write code that works with objects of different classes, as long as they implement the same interface.

Using polymorphism in Python

In Python, we can use polymorphism with any object that implements the same methods or has the same attributes. For example, we could write a function that takes a list of objects and calls a draw method on each of them, regardless of their class:

```
def draw_all(objects):
    for obj in objects:
        obj.draw()
```

Here, the draw_all function takes a list of objects and calls the draw method on each of them. As long as each object has a draw method, this function will work correctly.

Polymorphism in Inheritance

In the context of object-oriented programming, polymorphism refers to an object's capacity to adapt to different situations and take on multiple roles. This can be achieved through inheritance, where a child class inherits properties and methods from a parent class but can also modify or replace them to suit its specific requirements.

Overriding Methods

When a child class inherits from a parent class, it can override methods defined in the parent class by redefining them in the child class. This allows the child class to customize the behavior of inherited methods to suit its own needs. When a method is called on an instance of the child class, the method defined in the child class will be used instead of the method defined in the parent class.

For example, let's say we have a parent class called Animal with a method called speak():

```
class Animal:
    def speak(self):
        print("The animal speaks.")
```

Now, let's create a child class called Dog that inherits from the Animal class and overrides the speak() method:

```
class Dog(Animal):
    def speak(self):
        print("The dog barks.")
```

When we create an instance of the Dog class and call the speak() method, the method defined in the Dog class will be used:

```
>>> my_dog = Dog()
>>> my_dog.speak()
The dog barks.
```

This is an example of polymorphism in action. Even though my_dog is an instance of the Dog class, we can still call the speak() method on it because it inherits from the Animal class, which has a speak() method.

Using Super()

Sometimes, when overriding a method in a child class, we still want to use the behavior of the parent class's method in addition to some new behavior defined in the child class. We can do this using the super() function, which allows us to call a method defined in the parent class from within the child class.

For example, let's say we have a parent class called Shape with a method called area():

```
class Shape:
    def area(self):
```

```
        return 0
```

Now, let's create a child class called Square that inherits from the Shape class and overrides the area() method:

```
class Square(Shape):
    def __init__(self, side):
        self.side = side


    def area(self):
        # call the area() method from the parent
class using super()
        parent_area = super().area()
        return self.side * self.side + parent_area
```

When we create an instance of the Square class and call the area() method, we get the area of the square plus the value returned by the area() method of the parent class:

```
>>> my_square = Square(5)
>>> my_square.area()
25
```

In conclusion, inheritance and polymorphism are powerful features of object-oriented programming that allow us to create complex and flexible programs. By inheriting properties and methods from parent classes and overriding them in child classes, we can create objects that take on many forms and perform different actions depending on their current state. Polymorphism enables us to write code that can work with objects of different types, making our code more modular and reusable.

Practical Exercise: Building a Class Hierarchy

Let's gain some hands-on practice building out an object-oriented class hierarchy in Python:

1. Define a base Vehicle parent class with properties like make, model, year & methods start(), stop()
2. Create child classes Car and Truck inheriting from Vehicle

- Add extra properties like numDoors for Car and numAxels for Truck

3. Define capability methods in child classes:

- tow() in Truck to print "Towing in progress..."
- park() in Car to print "Parking car..."

4. Instantiate couple subclass objects like a camry = Car()

- Set model, year, doors and call park() & start()

5. Define a dealership list to contain mix of different vehicles

Some example usage would be:

```
python
 code
ram = Truck()
ram.make = "Dodge"
ram.tow() # Invokes subclass-specific method

parkedCars.append(Car()) # Polymorphically adds child
object
```

You now have practical hands-on experience leveraging key object oriented concepts like inheritance, subclasses and polymorphism to build out a custom class hierarchy that models a real-world system with logical classification.

Feel free to enhance this exercise further using other OOP principles covered in this chapter like encapsulation and abstraction.

Chapter 4: Advanced Topics

Python is a versatile language that can be used for a wide range of programming tasks. In this chapter, you will learn about some advanced topics in Python that can help you write more efficient, concise, and powerful code.

Regular Expressions

Regular expressions, commonly referred to as regex, are a potent means of identifying patterns in strings. They are composed of characters that establish a search pattern that can be utilized to locate and modify strings. Regular expressions provide the ability to conduct various tasks, including searching, replacing, and extracting data from text.

Overview of Regular Expressions:

Regular expressions are a valuable tool for finding patterns in strings. They are a set of characters that determine a search pattern. Regular expressions can be utilized to look for particular patterns in text, such as email addresses, phone numbers, or URLs.

Many programming languages, including Python, support regular expressions. The re module in Python is responsible for implementing regular expressions. It contains various functions for handling regular expressions, such as search(), match(), and findall().

Using Regular Expressions in Python:

Let's take a look at some examples of using regular expressions in Python.

Example 1: Matching a phone number

```
import re

phone_number = "555-1234"

# Use a regular expression to match the phone number
pattern
match = re.search(r'\d{3}-\d{4}', phone_number)

if match:
    print("Phone number found:", match.group())
else:
    print("Phone number not found")
```

```
Output:

Phone number found: 555-1234
```

In this example, we use the search() function from the re module to match a phone number pattern. The regular expression \d{3}-\d{4} matches a sequence of three digits, a hyphen, and four digits. If a match is found, we print the matched string using the group() method.

Example 2: Matching an email address

```
import re
email = "johndoe@example.com"

# Use a regular expression to match the email address
pattern
match = re.search(r'\w+@\w+\.\w+', email)

if match:
    print("Email address found:", match.group())
else:
    print("Email address not found")

Output:

Email address found: johndoe@example.com
```

In this example, we use the search() function again to match an email address pattern. The regular expression \w+@\w+\.\w+ matches a sequence of one or more word characters, an at symbol, one or more word characters, a period, and one or more word characters. If a match is found, we print the matched string using the group() method.

Lambda Functions

Lambda functions, also referred to as anonymous functions, are a functionality provided by several programming languages which allows the user to create small, temporary functions without specifying a name. These functions are usually used for operations such as filtering, mapping, or sorting data, and they are not defined in the traditional sense of a function with a name. Lambda functions are written in a concise, easy-to-read format and are often used in conjunction with other functions, such as filter() and map().

Introduction to Lambda Functions:

Lambda functions, also known as anonymous functions, are a way to create small, one-time use functions in Python. They are defined using the lambda keyword, followed by a list of arguments and an expression that is evaluated and returned.

Lambda functions are useful when you need to define a simple function quickly, without having to give it a name or define it elsewhere in your code.

Using Lambda Functions in Python:

Let's take a look at some examples of using lambda functions in Python.

Example 1: Squaring a number

```
square = lambda x: x**2
print(square(5))

Output:
25
```

In this example, a lambda function is used to calculate the square of a number. The lambda function is assigned to a variable named "square", and is called with an argument of 5 using the print() function. The output of this code is the number 25.

Example 2: Sorting a list of tuples

```
fruits = [('apple', 3), ('banana', 2),('orange', 4)]
```

```
Output:

[('banana', 2), ('apple', 3), ('orange', 4)]
```

In this example, we define a list of tuples containing fruit names and their corresponding quantities. We use a lambda function as the key argument to the sorted() function. The lambda function takes a tuple as its argument and returns the second element of the tuple (the quantity). This causes the list to be sorted based on the quantities of each fruit.

List Comprehensions

List comprehensions are a concise way of creating lists in many programming languages. They allow you to create a list using a single line of code, without the need for loops or complex expressions. With list comprehensions, you can filter, map, and apply functions to elements in a list in a single line of code.

Creating Lists with List Comprehensions:

List comprehensions are a concise way to create lists in Python. They allow you to define a list using a single line of code, instead of using a loop to append each item to the list.

List comprehensions consist of three parts: an expression, a variable, and a sequence. For each item in the sequence, the expression is computed and the variable is assigned the value of that item in every iteration.

Example 1: Squaring a list of numbers

```
numbers = [1, 2, 3, 4, 5]

squares = [x**2 for x in numbers]

print(squares)
```

```
Output:

[1, 4, 9, 16, 25]
```

In this example, we use a list comprehension to create a new list of the squares of the numbers in the original list. The expression x**2 is evaluated for each value of x in the numbers list.

Advanced List Comprehension Techniques:

List comprehensions can be nested and combined with conditional expressions to create more complex lists.

Example 2: Flattening a list of lists

```
matrix = [[1, 2, 3], [4, 5, 6], [7, 8, 9]]

flatten = [num for row in matrix for num in row]

print(flatten)

Output:

[1, 2, 3, 4, 5, 6, 7, 8, 9]
```

In this example, we use a nested list comprehension to flatten a list of lists. The outer comprehension iterates over each row in the matrix list, and the inner comprehension iterates over each number in each row. The resulting list contains all the numbers from the original list, in order.

Decorators

Decorators in Python provide a way to change the behavior of functions or classes without altering the original code. These are essentially functions that take another function as input and return a modified version of it with added functionality.

Overview of Decorators in Python:

Decorators are a way to modify or enhance the behavior of functions in Python. Decorators provide a way to extend the behavior of a function or class without making any changes to the original code. They are created using the @ symbol followed by the name of the decorator function, which takes a function as an argument and returns a new modified version of that function.

Creating and Using Decorators:

Let's take a look at an example of creating and using a decorator in Python.

Example 1: Timing a function

```
import time


def time_it(func):
    def wrapper(*args, **kwargs):
        start = time.time()
        result = func(*args, **kwargs)
        end = time.time()
        print(f"{func.__name__} took {end -
start:.4f} seconds")
        return result
    return wrapper


@time_it
def slow_function():
    time.sleep(1)


slow_function()


Output:
```

```
slow_function took 1.0002 seconds
```

In this example, we define a decorator function called time_it. This decorator function accepts a function as input and returns a new function that calculates the execution time of the original function.

We then use the @time_it decorator syntax to apply the time_it decorator to the slow_function function. When we call slow_function(), the time_it decorator is automatically applied to the function, causing it to be timed when it is executed.

Generators

Generators are a feature in many programming languages that allow you to create iterators, which are objects that generate a sequence of values. Unlike lists, which generate all of their values at once, generators generate values on the fly, as they are requested. This makes them more memory-efficient for large data sets. Generators are often used for tasks such as generating random numbers, processing large files, and iterating over large data sets.

Overview of Generators in Python:

Generators are a type of iterable, like lists or tuples. However, unlike lists and tuples, generators do not store all of their values in memory at once. Instead, they generate each value on-the-fly as it is requested.

Generators are defined using a special syntax that includes the yield keyword. When a generator function is called, it returns an iterator object, but does not actually execute the function code until the iterator's __next__() method is called. Each time the yield keyword is encountered, the generator returns the current value and suspends execution, saving its state. When the iterator's __next__() method is called again, execution resumes from where it left off, and the next value is generated.

Creating and Using Generators:

Let's take a look at an example of creating and using a generator in Python.

Example 1: Generating Fibonacci numbers

```
def fibonacci():
    a, b = 0, 1
    while True:
        yield a
        a, b = b, a + b

fib = fibonacci()

for i in range(10):
    print(next(fib))

Output:

0
1
1
2
3
5
8
13
21
34
```

In this example, we define a generator function called fibonacci that generates the Fibonacci sequence. The generator function uses a while loop to repeatedly yield the current value of a, and then updates a and b to generate the next value.

We then create a generator object by calling fibonacci(), and use a for loop to iterate over the first 10 values of the sequence. Each value is generated on-the-fly as it is requested by the next() function.

In this chapter, we covered several advanced topics in Python, including regular expressions, lambda functions, list comprehensions, decorators, and generators. Regular expressions are used to match patterns in strings using a specific syntax. Lambda functions are a way to write short, one-line functions without naming them. List comprehensions are a concise way to create lists in Python and can be nested and combined with conditional expressions to create more complex lists. Decorators let you change how functions behave in Python without altering the original function code. Lastly, generators enable you to create values as they are requested, instead of storing all values in memory at once. By mastering these advanced topics, you can become a more proficient and versatile Python programmer.

BOOK 2

Python Libraries and Tools

James P. Meyers

Chapter 1: Python Libraries and Applications

Python is an effective programming language that comes packaged with a sizable collection of frameworks and libraries to choose from. In this chapter, we will investigate some of the most well-known Python libraries and applications, such as NumPy, Pandas, Matplotlib, Flask, and Django. These are just a few examples.

Python Standard Libraries with Codes

The Python Standard Library is a vast collection of modules that come pre-installed with Python. These modules provide a wide range of functionalities, from mathematical operations and file handling to internet protocols and web service tools. Below, I'll introduce a few commonly used modules with example codes for each:

math - Mathematical Functions

The math module provides access to the mathematical functions defined by the C standard.

```python
python
    import math

    # Calculate the square root
    print(math.sqrt(16))

    # Trigonometric functions
    print(math.sin(math.pi / 2))

    # Constants
    print(math.pi)
```

datetime - Date and Time Handling

The datetime module supplies classes for manipulating dates and times.

```python
python
    from datetime import datetime, timedelta

    # Current date and time
    now = datetime.now()
    print(now)

    # Date one week from now
    one_week_later = now + timedelta(weeks=1)
    print(one_week_later)

    # Formatting date and time
    print(now.strftime('%Y-%m-%d %H:%M:%S'))
```

random - Generate Pseudo-random Numbers

The random module is used to perform random actions such as generating random numbers.

```python
import random

# Random float number between 0 and 1
print(random.random())

# Random integer between 1 and 10
print(random.randint(1, 10))

# Choose a random element from a list
print(random.choice(['apple', 'banana',
'cherry']))
```

statistics - Mathematical Statistic Functions

The statistics module provides functions for calculating mathematical statistics of numeric data.

Example: Calculating Mean, Median, and Standard Deviation

```python
import statistics

data = [1, 2, 3, 4, 5]

mean = statistics.mean(data)
median = statistics.median(data)
stdev = statistics.stdev(data)
```

```
print(f'Mean: {mean}')
print(f'Median: {median}')
print(f'Standard Deviation: {stdev}')
```

string - String Operations

The string module contains a collection of string operations and constants.

Example: String Constants and Capwords

```
python
    import string

    # Example of string constants
    print(string.ascii_letters)
    print(string.digits)

    # Capwords function to capitalize words in a
    string
    s = 'hello world'
    cap_s = string.capwords(s)

    print(cap_s)
```

re - Regular Expression Operations

The re module provides support for regular expressions, allowing for complex string searching and manipulation.

Example: Searching and Replacing Text

```
python
    import re

    text = "Python is fun"
```

```
pattern = 'Python'

# Check if pattern is present in text
if re.search(pattern, text):
    print('Found Python!')

# Replace 'Python' with 'Programming'
new_text = re.sub(pattern, 'Programming', text)
print(new_text)
```

collections - Container Data Types

The collections module offers specialized container datatypes providing alternatives to Python's general-purpose built-in containers.

Example: Using defaultdict and Counter

```
python
    from collections import defaultdict, Counter

    # defaultdict example
    dd = defaultdict(int)
    dd['apple'] += 1
    print(dd['apple'])  # Output: 1
    print(dd['banana'])  # Output: 0, default value

    # Counter example
    fruits = ['apple', 'banana', 'cherry', 'apple',
    'cherry']
    fruit_count = Counter(fruits)
    print(fruit_count)  # Output: Counter({'apple':
    2, 'cherry': 2, 'banana': 1})
```

NumPy

NumPy, which stands for "Numerical Python," is a Python library that is available for anybody to use and is used in almost every area of research and engineering. It is the gold standard for dealing with numerical data in Python, and it is at the center of the ecosystems for scientific Python and PyData. Users of NumPy range from novice programmers to seasoned researchers engaged in cutting-edge scientific and commercial R&D. NumPy users conduct cutting-edge research and development in a variety of fields. The NumPy Application Programming Interface (API) is heavily used in most of the other Python packages used for data science and scientific research, including Pandas, SciPy, Matplotlib, scikit-learn, and scikit-image.

Data structures in the form of multidimensional arrays and matrices may be found in the NumPy package. It gives the ndarray object, which is a homogenous n-dimensional array, with methods that may operate on it in an efficient manner. Arrays are a good candidate for NumPy's ability to execute a broad range of mathematical operations on them. It extends Python with powerful data structures that ensure accurate computations when working with arrays and matrices, and it provides a sizable library of high-level mathematical functions that can be used on arrays and matrices. These functions can be used to perform operations on the arrays and matrices.

Overview of NumPy:

NumPy is a library for Python that provides support for huge, multi-dimensional arrays and matrices, in addition to a large number of high-level mathematical functions that can be used to work on these arrays. NumPy was developed by the NumPy project. In addition to its widespread applicability in scientific computing and data analysis, it serves as an indispensable instrument for a variety of machine learning and artificial intelligence tasks and programs.

Using NumPy for numerical computations:

NumPy offers a wide variety of functions that might be helpful when doing numerical calculations. For instance, it provides functions for computing fundamental mathematical operations such as adding, subtracting, multiplying, and dividing. Furthermore, it also provides functions for more complex mathematical operations such as multiplying matrices, decomposing eigenvalues, and performing Fourier transforms.

The ability to perform operations in a vectorized fashion is one of the most important aspects of NumPy. Instead of going through the process of iterating over each individual member of an array, you may conduct calculations on whole arrays at once with the help of vectorized operations. Especially when working with huge arrays, this may make a significant difference in the performance and efficiency of your code.

NumPy (Numerical Python) is an open source Python library used for scientific computing and working with large, multi-dimensional arrays and matrices. It includes a powerful N-dimensional array object and tools for integrating C/C++ code. NumPy has become an essential base package for data manipulation and analysis in fields like machine learning, finance, biology, physics, and more.

NumPy provides key advantages that make it popular for data analysis:

- Efficient handling of large arrays and matrices
- Vectorized functions for element-wise operations without Python loops
- Broadcasting for aligning arrays of different sizes during arithmetic operations
- Advanced mathematical and statistical functions
- Interoperability with hardware acceleration and libraries written in faster languages like C/C++

NumPy is commonly used alongside other Python data analysis libraries like Pandas and SciPy for specialized computing capabilities. It is supported by all major machine learning frameworks. NumPy enables concise, quicker to write, and more computationally efficient code than pure Python offers.

NumPy Arrays

The foundation of NumPy is the ndarray (N-dimensional array) class. These arrays are homogenous, storing elements of the same data type in a grid-like structure. This differs from Python lists which have no constraints on containing mixed types. Elements are accessed by their index like regular Python sequences.

Some key attributes of NumPy arrays:

- Fast mathematical operations from precompiled C code
- Efficient iteration and vectorized (element-wise) functions
- Support for advanced indexing and broadcasting
- Tools like masking for filtering data
- Integrated linear algebra, Fourier transform, and random number capabilities

Let's import NumPy and create our first array:

```
python
 code
import numpy as np


arr = np.array([1, 2, 3])
print(arr)


# Output
[1 2 3]
```

We pass Python's built-in list and get a NumPy array with the same elements. np is convention for importing NumPy.

NumPy Array Attributes

NumPy arrays have various attributes that facilitate working with multidimensional data interactively or programmatically:

```
python
 code
import numpy as np

arr = np.array([[1, 2, 3], [4, 5, 6]])

print(arr.shape) # Dimensionality
# (2, 3) - 2 rows, 3 columns

print(arr.dtype) # Data type of elements
# int64 - 64-bit integer

print(arr.size) # Total number of elements
# 6

print(arr.ndim) # Number of dimensions
# 2
```

These attributes help while inspecting arrays in code or for automated processing in production pipelines. randint, zeros and ones are useful factory methods for sample arrays.

```
python
 code
import numpy as np
```

```
arr = np.zeros((2, 4)) # 2 rows, 4 columns with 0s
print(arr)

arr = np.ones((3, 3)) # 3x3 array of 1s
print(arr)

arr = np.randint(0, 10, (3, 3)) # Random ints
print(arr)
```

Array Indexing

NumPy makes array manipulation intuitive through indexing. Elements can be accessed singly or in slices:

```
python
 code
import numpy as np

arr = np.array([1, 2, 3, 4, 5, 6, 7])

print(arr[3]) # 4

slice_arr = arr[1:5]
print(slice_arr) # [2 3 4 5]

# Setting values
arr[0] = 0
print(arr) # [0 2 3 4 5 6 7]
```

Indexing also works for multidimensional arrays using tuples:

```
python
```

```
code
arr_2d = np.array([[5, 10, 15], [20, 25, 30]])

print(arr_2d[1, 2]) # 30 - 2nd row, 3rd column

arr_2d[0, 1] = 50  # Assign new value
print(arr_2d)
```

NumPy arrays facilitate advanced indexing like conditional filtering, permutation, and more.

Array Operations

Performing math on arrays applies the operation element-wise:

```
python
 code
import numpy as np

arr = np.array([1, 2, 3, 4])
print(arr + 2) # Add 2 to each element

arr = np.array([[1, 1], [0, 1]])
print(arr * 10) # Multiply each element by 10
```

This vectorization makes NumPy fast for numerical routines without Python for-loops.

Basic statistics across an array like min, max and mean are handy:

```
python
 code
import numpy as np

arr = np.array([[1,3,5], [4,7,9]])
```

```
print(arr.min()) # 1
print(arr.max()) # 9
print(arr.mean()) # 5
```

```
NumPy has full linear algebra operations:
python
 code
import numpy as np

matrix = np.array([[1,1], [0,1]])
vector = np.array([2, 1])

vector_product = np.dot(matrix, vector)
print(vector_product)

matrix_mult = np.dot(matrix, matrix)
print(matrix_mult)
```

Broadcasting is a powerful concept that aligns arrays of different sizes during operations:

```
python
 code
import numpy as np

arr_1 = np.array([[1, 2], [3, 4]])
arr_2 = np.array([10, 20])

print(arr_1 * arr_2) # [[10 40]
                     # [30 80]]
```

Here arr_2 works with arr_1 due to broadcasting.

There are many more NumPy capabilities we have not covered like aggregations, sorting, reshaping, histograms, load/save from disk and more. NumPy forms the starting point for many areas of Python data analysis and scientific computing.

NumPy Exercises

Exercise 1

Import NumPy under the namespace 'np' and print the version number.

Exercise 2

Create a 3x3 ndarray with all values set to 1.

Multiply this array by 5 using vectorization and print the result.

Exercise 3

Generate a 5x5 array with random float values between 0 and 1. Find the minimum, maximum, mean, standard deviation, and sum of the values.

Pandas

Pandas is an open-source library that is primarily designed for dealing with relational or labeled data in an easy and natural manner. Its primary purpose is to facilitate this kind of work. It offers a wide variety of data structures and operations that may be used to manipulate numerical data and time series. The NumPy library serves as the foundation for this library's construction. Pandas is very quick, and it provides users with exceptional performance and productivity.

Overview of Pandas

Pandas gives users access to a wide variety of methods for dealing with DataFrames, such as routines for importing data from CSV files, SQL databases, and other sources. In addition to this, it contains methods for cleaning and converting data, such as functions for deleting missing values, integrating data from various sources, and filtering data based on certain criteria.

Pandas' support for many types of data visualization is one of its most important features. It simplifies the process of exploring and visualizing huge datasets by providing methods for the creation of plots and charts that are based on the data contained in a DataFrame.

Pandas is a package for the Python programming language that offers data structures that are quick, versatile, and expressive. Its purpose is to simplify and streamline the process of dealing with "relational" or "labeled" data. Its goal is to become the most basic and high-level building block for conducting realistic, real-world data analysis in Python. In addition to this, its overarching objective is to become into the most effective and adaptable open-source data analysis and manipulation tool that is currently accessible in any language. It has already made significant progress in achieving this objective.

Pandas is adaptable to a wide variety of data types, including the following:

Data presented in a tabular format containing columns of varying data types, such as those seen in a SQL table or an Excel spreadsheet

both sorted and unordered time series data, with the frequency not necessarily being set.

Data in an arbitrary matrix, either of a homogeneous type or of a heterogeneous kind, with row and column labels

Every other kind of observational or statistical data collection there is. Putting the data into a Pandas data structure does not in any way need the data to be labeled.

Both the Series (1-dimensional) and DataFrame (2-dimensional) basic data structures of the pandas programming language are capable of handling the great majority of the normal use cases that arise in the fields of finance, statistics, social science, and many branches of engineering. DataFrame offers all of R's data to users of the R programming language. frame supplies all of these things and much more. pandas is designed to work nicely inside a scientific computing environment with a large number of different third party libraries. It was created on top of NumPy and is designed with this integration in mind.

The following is a short list of the many things that pandas are good at:

With both floating point and non-floating point data, the management of missing data, which is represented by the symbol NaN, is made simple.

- Modifiability of size: columns may be added to or removed from DataFrames and higher-dimensional objects.
- Automatic and explicit data alignment: The Pandas library provides automatic and explicit data alignment, allowing objects to be aligned to a set of labels. It also allows users to disregard labels and rely on the library's data structure alignment during computations.

Pandas also offers split-apply-combine functionality to perform operations on data sets with flexible group-by capabilities. This feature enables both aggregation and transformation of data.

Make it simple to transform sloppy, inconsistently indexed data stored in existing Python and NumPy data structures into objects that can be used with DataFrame.

Large-scale data sets may benefit from intelligent label-based slicing, fancy indexing, and subsetting.

Intuitive merging and connecting data sets

Data sets may be reshaped and rotated in a flexible manner.

Axes that are labeled in a hierarchical fashion (possible to have multiple labels per tick)

Powerful input/output (IO) facilities for loading data from flat files (both CSV and delimited), Excel files, and databases, as well as storing and loading data from the very fast HDF5 format.

Functionality unique to time series, including date range creation and frequency conversion; moving window statistics; date shifting and lagging; and date lagging.

A significant number of these concepts were developed in order to solve the inadequacies that are typically encountered while using other languages or scientific research settings. Working with data is often broken down into various steps when it is done by data scientists. These processes include: munging and cleaning the data, analyzing and modeling it, and then putting the findings of the analysis into a form that is appropriate for charting or tabular presentation. Pandas is the tool that excels at all of these responsibilities.

A few other observations

Pandas move quite quickly. A significant number of the low-level algorithmic components have undergone major modification in the code written in Cython. Unfortunately, as is the case with most things, generality almost always comes at the expense of performance. If you zero down on a single function for your application, you will likely be able to develop a more efficient and focused tool.

pandas is an essential component of Python's environment for statistical computing as a result of its status as a dependent of the statsmodels package.

Pandas has had a significant amount of production usage in the field of financial applications.

Using Pandas for data manipulation and analysis:

Pandas provides many functions for working with DataFrames, including functions for loading data from CSV files, SQL databases, and other sources. It also provides functions for cleaning and transforming data, including functions for removing missing values, merging data from multiple sources, and filtering data based on specific criteria.

One of the key features of Pandas is its support for data visualization. It provides functions for creating plots and charts based on the data in a DataFrame, making it easy to explore and visualize large datasets.

Pandas provides high performance, easy to use data structures and data analysis tools for Python. It is tailored specifically for working with tabular or structured data in an intuitive way. Pandas is well suited for finance, statistics, social sciences, and anything requiring data manipulation or analysis. It has become essential for data science workflows.

The Pandas library key features include:

- Intuitive data structures - Series (1D) and DataFrames (2D) for working with data
- Integrates well with NumPy arrays
- Tools for reading and writing data between various file formats and databases
- Vectorized string operations for text data manipulation
- Timeseries specific functionality such as date range generation and frequency conversions
- Powerful indexing for slicing and dicing data
- Merging, joining, grouping, pivoting and shaping of datasets
- Easy handling of missing data via NaN values

- Rich statistics methods, summarization, aggregation, and visualization

With this versatile toolkit, Pandas helps you get productive analyzing data quickly. It abstracts away tedious details around working with tabular and time series data at scale.

Pandas Series

The Pandas Series is a one-dimensional, array-like structure designed to handle and label sequences of data. It builds on NumPy arrays with customized indexing. Let's make one from scratch:

```
python
 code
import pandas as pd
import numpy as np

data = np.array(['1', '2', '3'])
s = pd.Series(data)

print(s)
# Output:
0    1
1    2
2    3
dtype: object
```

A Pandas Series wraps data with an index for label-based access. Common factory functions like those using dictionaries are more convenient:

```
python
 code
data = {'Band': 'Beatles', 'Year': 1964, 'Hits': 'A
Hard Days Night'}
```

```
s = pd.Series(data)

print(s['Band']) # Beatles
print(s[0]) # Beatles
```

Pandas Series have array-oriented capabilities like other Python sequence types alongside customized features like indexing, reshaping, grouping, and more. They serve as building blocks for DataFrames.

Pandas DataFrames

A Pandas DataFrame represents 2D tabular data with rows and columns. It can be created from nested Python dictionaries or lists:

```
python
 code
data = {
  'Name': ['John', 'Steve', 'Sarah'],
    'Age': [28, 32, 25],
    'City': ['New York', 'Los Angeles', 'Chicago']
}

df = pd.DataFrame(data)
print(df)
#        Name  Age        City
# 0     John   28     New York
# 1    Steve   32  Los Angeles
# 2    Sarah   25      Chicago
```

We have column labels and an index generated automatically from 0 to number of rows minus 1. There are several DataFrame creation helpers for cases like reading CSV and JSON files.

Dataframe Indexing

Pandas indexing provides expressive ways to subset and query dataframes leveraging labels and positions:

```
python
 code
print(df['Name'])
# 0     John
# 1    Steve
# 2    Sarah
# Name: Name, dtype: object

print(df.loc[0])
# Name      John
# Age         28
# City      New York
# Name: 0, dtype: object
```

DataFrames have columnar, row and scalar value accessors like df.Column, df.loc[], df.at[] and df.iat[]. Square brackets slice rows/columns similar to NumPy arrays.

Boolean indexing filters rows meeting logical criteria:

```
python
 code
drop_rows = df[df['Age'] > 30]
print(drop_rows)
```

Expressive Pandas indexing and querying comes in handy for data exploration and analysis.

Handling Missing Data

Pandas uses NumPy nan values to handle missing data. This avoids unintended upcasts to float that using None would incur.

```
python
 code
vals1 = [1, None, 3, 4]
vals2 = [1, np.nan, 3, 4]

print(type(pd.Series(vals1))) # floats
print(type(pd.Series(vals2))) # integers
```

We can fill missing values with .fillna(), drop rows/columns with nulls using .dropna(), or interpolate missing data with .interpolate(). This flexibility helps address incomplete datasets.

Dataframe Operations

Pandas inherits vectorization from NumPy enabling element-wise operations instead of slow Python loops:

```
python
 code
df = pd.DataFrame({
    'Data': [1, 2, 3],
    'Values': [10, 20, 30]
})

df['Doubled'] = df['Values'] * 2 # Vectorized
print(df)

#    Data  Values  Doubled
# 0     1      10       20
```

```
# 1      2        20        40
# 2      3        30        60
```

Timeseries specific capabilities help when working with date data:

```
python
 code
dates = pd.date_range('2020-01-01', periods=3,
freq='M')

df = pd.DataFrame({
    'Num': [1, 2, 3],
    'Date': dates
})

print(df)
#     Num       Date
# 0     1 2020-01-31
# 1     2 2020-02-29
# 2     3 2020-03-31

print(df.set_index('Date')) # Datetime indexing
```

Pandas has operators, methods, and logic providing an analytics toolkit on tabular data leveraging vectorization.

Data Aggregation

Pandas aggregates along Series/DataFrames with .sum(), .mean(), .count() etc for summary statistics:

```
python
 code
students = {
```

```
    'Name': ['Sarah', 'John', 'Steve'],
    'Grade': [98, 87, 92]
}

df = pd.DataFrame(students)

all_grades = df['Grade'].sum() # Total of all grades
print(all_grades)

avg_grade = df['Grade'].mean() # Average grade
print(avg_grade)
```

More complex aggregations like groupby are useful across cohorts:

python

code

```
by_class = df.groupby('Grade').agg({
    'Name': 'count', # Number of students
    'Grade': 'min' # Minimum grade
})

print(by_class)
#       Name  Grade
# Grade
# 87       1     87
# 92       1     92
# 98       1     98
```

With its data structures, analysis methods and I/O capabilities, Pandas makes Python fully equipped for production-ready, flexible data processing.

Pandas Exercises

Exercise 1

Generate a series from the list [5, 3, 6, 4, 7] and print the output.

Exercise 2

Given this data, create a dataframe with columns Name and Age:

```
Name=['Jason', 'Molly' , 'Tina', 'Jake', 'Amy']
    Age=[42, 52, 36, 24, 73]
```

Print the dataframe.

Exercise 3

Take the dataframe from Exercise 2. Add a new column called Discount that holds 10% of the Age.

Print the updated dataframe.

Matplotlib

When it comes to the display of data, one of the most often used Python libraries is called Matplotlib. It is a library that works on several platforms and can generate 2D graphs from data stored in arrays. Matplotlib is built in Python and makes use of NumPy, which is an extension of Python that specializes in numerical mathematics. It offers an object-oriented API that makes it easier to integrate plots in programs written in Python and that use graphical user interface toolkits like PyQt, WxPython, or Tkinter. It is also compatible with the IPython shell and the Python shell, as well as the Jupyter notebook and web application servers.

A procedural interface known as the Pylab is included in Matplotlib. This interface is supposed to be analogous to MATLAB, which is a proprietary programming language produced by MathWorks. It's possible that Matplotlib and NumPy, when used together, might be thought of as the open source version of MATLAB.

Overview of Matplotlib:

Matplotlib is a library for Python that offers a comprehensive set of tools for the generation of data visualizations of the highest possible quality. It offers a variety of plotting features, such as line plots, scatter plots, bar charts, and more, and is extensively used in scientific computing, data analysis, and machine learning.

Creating data visualizations with Matplotlib:

Matplotlib is a collection of functions that may be used to create many types of data visualizations. These functions can be used to create line plots, scatter plots, histograms, and many more. It also has methods for modifying the look of plots, including the ability to change the color, the size of the text, and other properties.

The capability of Matplotlib to generate interactive graphs is one of its most notable and useful capabilities. It has utilities for constructing graphs that can be zoomed, panned, and rotated, which makes it simple to investigate enormous datasets in more depth.

Matplotlib is the most popular Python 2D plotting library used for visualizing data, enabling data exploration, and assisting in data analysis. It produces a wide range of charts and graphs with publication quality. The PyPlot interface provides a MATLAB-style API generating plots using Python scripts or the interactive shell.

Matplotlib capabilities include:

- A wide range of 2D plot types - line, bar, scatter, histogram etc
- Extremely customizable across chart elements
- Support for special chart types like contour, polar plots and heatmaps
- Integrated well with NumPy and Pandas data structures
- Can export charts in all standard formats - JPEG, PNG, TIFF etc

- Backends to generate vector graphics like PDF or SVG

Due to this versatility, Matplotlib is used across domains - finance, medicine, engineering, data science etc. Let's import matplotlib and Numpy:

```
python
 code
import matplotlib.pyplot as plt
import numpy as np
```

By convention matplotlib.pyplot is imported as 'plt'. Numpy helps generate data.

Basic XY Plot

The most basic Matplotlib chart is the line plot created by the plot function. It takes two arrays - X values and Y values:

```
python
 code
x = np.arange(0, 10)
y = x

plt.plot(x, y)
plt.xlabel('X Label')
plt.ylabel('Y Label')
plt.title('Simple XY Plot')
plt.show()
```

This plots a diagonal straight line. Matplotlib analyzes the numbers and interpolates/smooths the line. Ticks, gridlines and labels contextualize the data.

Many options like color, line style, width etc can customize the plot:

```
python
 code
x = np.arange(0, 10)
y = x

plt.plot(x, y, color='red', lw=5, ls='--',
marker='o')

plt.title('Customized XY Plot')
plt.show()
```

Here red thicker dashed line, circle markers and no gridlines alter the chart's look.

Bar Charts

Bar charts represent categorical data with rectangle bars proportional to values. Heights given by a sequence:

```
python
 code
values = [100, 600, 250, 400]
labels = ['A', 'B', 'C', 'D']

plt.bar(labels, values)
plt.title('Bar Chart')
plt.show()
```

We can control bar width, orientation, color and more for effective comparisons.

Histograms

Histograms visualize distributions by bucketing values into ranges (bins). freq of occurrences within each bin is plotted:

```
python
 code
values = np.random.normal(size=1000) # Random normal


plt.hist(values)
plt.title('Histogram')
plt.show()
```

This plots a bell curve like distribution given the normal data. Custom bin sizing, alignments etc enable tweaking histograms.

Scatter Plots

Scatter plots visualize relationships between two numeric variables as points spaced by x and y coordinates:

```
python
 code
x = np.arange(10)
y = x * 2


plt.scatter(x, y, color='red', marker='+')


plt.title('Scatter Plot')
plt.show()
```

Data points are marked, often differentiated by categories through colors, symbols etc. Useful for cluster analysis.

Figures and Subplots

Matplotlib subplots enable multiple plots in a single figure in grid arrangements:

```
python
 code
# Plot 1
x1 = [1, 3, 5]
y1 = [4, 8, 2]

# Plot 2
x2 = [2, 4, 6]
y2 = [3, 1, 5]

# Figure
fig, (ax1, ax2) = plt.subplots(1, 2)

ax1.plot(x1, y1)
ax1.set_title('Plot 1')

ax2.scatter(x2, y2, color='red')
ax2.set_title('Plot 2')

fig.suptitle('Figure with 2 Subplots')
plt.show()
```

Adjusting figure size, subplots, spacing and layouts crafts complex charts.

There are many more plot types like pie charts, area plots, heatmaps etc. Matplotlib empowers all data visualization needs.

Matplotlib Exercises

Exercise 1

Use Matplotlib to plot a simple line chart with x values ranging from 1-10 and y values as x^2. Apply red circles for plot markers.

Exercise 2

Plot two bar charts side by side - one showing five technology companies by revenue, other showing user counts for leading social apps. Apply custom color scheme.

Exercise 3

Plot a histogram visualizing the frequency distribution of heights (in cm) for 100 students. Specify 8 bins from 140 cm to 200 cm.

Flask

Flask is a popular web application framework that allows developers to quickly build and deploy web applications using Python. It is known for its simplicity and flexibility, making it a great choice for small to medium-sized projects. Flask provides a simple and easy-to-use API for handling HTTP requests, and it supports a wide range of extensions and plugins that allow developers to add functionality to their applications.

Building web applications with Flask

To get started with Flask, developers need to install the Flask library using pip, the Python package manager. Once Flask is installed, developers can create a new Flask application by defining a Python module and using the Flask class to create a new instance of the application.

From there, developers can define routes, which map URLs to Python functions that handle the request. Flask provides a simple and intuitive API for handling HTTP requests, making it easy to build a basic web application in just a few lines of code.

Flask also supports a wide range of extensions and plugins that allow developers to add functionality to their applications. For example, developers can use Flask-WTF to handle form submissions, Flask-SQLAlchemy to work with databases, or Flask-Login to handle user authentication.

Overview of Flask

Flask was first released in 2010 by Armin Ronacher and has since become one of the most popular web frameworks for Python. Flask is a micro-framework, which means that it is designed to be lightweight and flexible, allowing developers to choose only the components they need for their project.

Flask is designed to be simple and straightforward, providing developers with only the essential tools and libraries required for building web applications. This approach enables developers to concentrate on writing code rather than setting up the application. Additionally, Flask comes with a development server built-in, which simplifies the process of testing and debugging applications locally.

Flask is a popular, lightweight Python web application framework. It is classified as a microframework as it does not have built-in abstraction layers for databases, schemas etc but instead has third-party extensions providing that functionality. Flask gives flexibility and fine-grained control compared to batteries included full-stack frameworks.

Below are some notable features of Flask:

- Lightweight with minimal dependencies - easy to get started
- Embedded development server and debugger
- RESTful request routing using Python decorators
- Template engine integration supporting Jinja, React etc
- Compatibility with databases like MySQL, Postgres etc

- Extensible with myriad WSGI features and plugins
- Active community and ecosystem

Flask promotes simplicity, flexibility and fine-grained control ideal for websites, prototypes and web services. Large companies like LinkedIn and Pinterest use Flask behind the scenes.

Basic Application

A simple Flask app looks like:

```
python
 code
from flask import Flask

app = Flask(__name__)

@app.route('/')
def home():
    return 'Hello, Flask!'

if __name__ == '__main__':
   app.run(debug=True)
```

app is the central Flask object. @app.route maps URLs to view functions. Running this provides a working example at http://localhost:5000.

Request and Response

The view uses request parameters and returns response data:

```
python
 code
from flask import request
```

```
@app.route('/profile/<username>')
def profile(username):
    data = f'Profile for: {username}'
    return data
```

http://localhost:5000/profile/john - Custom endpoints are that easy!

We can render templates to build complete pages:

```
python
 code
from flask import render_template

@app.route('/about')
def about():
    return render_template('about.html')
```

Templates are stored separately under /templates folder or custom location.

Application Structure

As Flask apps scale, we refactor for better structure:

```
 code
app.py # Central app object, config
views.py # Route handlers
models.py # Database models

templates/
  index.html
  base.html

static/
```

```
  style.css
  main.js
```

Initialization code moves to app.py. Shared logic in dedicated files avoids duplication.

Database Integration

Flask integrates SQLAlchemy for database ORM capabilities:

```
python
 code
from flask_sqlalchemy import SQLAlchemy


app = Flask(__name__)
db = SQLAlchemy(app)


class User(db.Model):
  id = db.Column(db.Integer, primary_key=True)
  name = db.Column(db.String(80))
Std ORM operations like insert, query available:
python
 code
user = User(name='Susan')
db.session.add(user)
db.session.commit()


print(User.query.get(1).name) # Susan
```

Many extensions like Flask-MySQL, Flask-Migrate handle other database/app needs.

Flask empowers building scalable, production-grade sites and web services with its expansive ecosystem.

Flask Exercises

Exercise 1

Create a simple Flask application displaying 'Hello World!'. Run the development server and view it locally.

Exercise 2

Create a route /profile that takes name as a URL parameter and returns content like: <p>Profile page for: <b>John</b></p>

Exercise 3

Use Flask's render_template method to render an HTML template called home.html containing markup for the homepage.

Django

Django is a full-stack web application framework that allows developers to build complex web applications quickly and easily using Python. It is known for its robustness, scalability, and security, making it a popular choice for building large-scale web applications.

Overview of Django

Django was first released in 2005 by a group of developers at Lawrence Journal-World newspaper. Since then, it has become one of the most popular web frameworks for Python, used by companies like Instagram, Pinterest, and Mozilla.

Django is a batteries-included framework, which means that it comes with a wide range of tools and libraries for building web applications, including an ORM for working with databases, a built-in admin interface, and a powerful templating system.

Building web applications with Django

To get started with Django, developers need to install the Django library using pip. Once Django is installed, developers can create a new Django project using the django-admin command-line utility.

From there, developers can define models, which represent the data in their application, and use the Django ORM to interact with the database. Django also provides a powerful templating system for rendering HTML pages, and a built-in admin interface that makes it easy to manage the data in the application.

Django also supports a wide range of third-party packages and plugins, allowing developers to add functionality to their applications quickly and easily. For example, developers can use Django Rest Framework to build RESTful APIs, or Django Allauth to handle user authentication and registration.

Python is a highly adaptable and dynamic programming language that can be utilized in diverse domains such as scientific computation and web development. Throughout this chapter, we have examined some of the most widely used frameworks and libraries in Python such as NumPy, Pandas, Matplotlib, Flask, and Django.

Each of these tools has its own advantages and limitations, and selecting the most suitable one for your project will depend on the specific demands and criteria. However, by learning how to use these tools effectively, you can greatly improve your productivity and the quality of your work.

By using NumPy, you can perform complex numerical computations with ease, whether it's in the fields of data science, engineering, or finance. Pandas, on the other hand, is a powerful tool for data manipulation and analysis, allowing you to easily clean, transform, and analyze data sets of all sizes and shapes.

If you need to create visualizations to better understand your data or to present your findings to others, Matplotlib provides a wide range of options to create professional-grade charts and graphs.

For web development, Flask and Django are two popular frameworks that offer different approaches to building web applications. Flask is a micro web framework that is lightweight and flexible, making it ideal for small to medium-sized projects. Django, on the other hand, is a full-stack web framework that comes with many built-in features and tools to make web development faster and easier.

Django is an extremely popular open source web application framework written in Python. It enables rapid development and clean, pragmatic design of websites ranging from simple to complex. Django follows a model-template-views architectural pattern.

Key aspects that make Django highly effective:

- Includes an object-relational mapper (ORM) providing an abstraction layer above the database
- Follows the don't repeat yourself (DRY) principle so no duplication of code and logic
- Packaged with common tools like admin screens, caching etc out of the box
- Highly opinionated structure leading to standardization
- Focused on automating tedious work allowing quicker development cycles
- Security conscious with protection against many vulnerabilities

Django helps create robust production-grade web applications. Companies like Instagram, Spotify, YouTube use Django behind the scenes. The ecosystem provides libraries and extensions for needs like API building, machine learning etc.

Project Setup

It is best practice to run each Django project in its own isolated environment. We will use Python virtualenv:

```
bash
 code
$ python3 -m venv env
$ source env/bin/activate
```

Now install Django and create a new project:

```
bash
 code
$ pip install Django==3.2


$ django-admin startproject first_project
$ cd first_project
```

This provides a starter skeleton. Let's run the development server:

```
bash
 code
$ python manage.py runserver
```

By default at http://localhost:8000/ we get a running site.

Django Apps

Django encourages modular applications making projects extensible. An app holds a specific functionality - polls, blog etc:

```
bash
 code
$ python manage.py startapp blog


$ ls -1 blog/
__init__.py models.py views.py  # And more
```

Reference blog's config in main settings. Now blog elements reside under their own namespace.

Models and Database

Django's object-relational mapper (ORM) generates SQL behind the scenes. We define data models in Python without raw SQL:

```
python
 code
# blog/models.py

from django.db import models

class Post(models.Model):
    title = models.CharField(max_length=100)
    content = models.TextField()
    published_date = models.DateField(auto_now_
add=True)
```

To sync models to the database:

```
bash
 code
$ python manage.py migrate
# Applies migrations and creates database schema
```

Now scripts can import and manipulate Post objects through generated APIs without SQL.

Views and Templates

A view handles one page's request/response. Templates render page HTML.

```
python
 code
# blog/views.py
from django.shortcuts import render
```

```
def home(request):
    posts = Post.objects.all()
    return render(request, 'home.html', {'posts':
posts})
```

Template loaded by the view:

```
html
 code
<!-- home.html -->

{% for post in posts %}
<h1>{{ post.title }}</h1>
<p>{{ post.content }}</p>
{% endfor %}
```

Templates dynamically inject Python data into markup also supporting logic and inheritance.

The URL dispatcher connects views to actual URLs:

```
python
 code
# first_project/urls.py

from django.urls import path
from blog import views

urlpatterns = [
  path('', views.home, name='blog_home'),
]
```

Now http://localhost:8000 loads the home page view and template.

Admin Interface

Django can auto generate admin screens for managing content. After registering models with the admin, it provides a production-ready interface.

```
python
 code
# blog/admin.py


from django.contrib import admin
from .models import Post


admin.site.register(Post)
```

Now we can visit http://localhost:8000/admin and log into the auto created UI for creating blog posts without coding an interface from scratch!

Django Exercises

Exercise 1

Create a new Django project called blog_project. Generate requirements.txt file with project dependencies.

Exercise 2

Inside blog_project, start a new app called articles. Create a simple Article model with title and content fields.

Exercise 3

Register Article model with admin. Initialize database tables. Start server and access admin to add test articles.

In conclusion, Python's popularity and versatility can be attributed in part to its extensive library ecosystem, which provides developers with a vast array of tools and frameworks to accomplish almost any task. Whether you're a data scientist, software engineer, or web developer, there is likely a Python library or framework that can help you achieve your goals. By learning how to use these tools effectively, you can not only improve your own productivity but also create higher quality and more powerful applications.

Practical Exercise: Data Analysis with NumPy and Pandas

This exercise walks through a practical data analysis task leveraging foundational Python data analysis tools - NumPy and Pandas.

We will:

1. Load and explore a real world datasets
2. Wrangle the data into an analysis-friendly structure
3. Analyze data for insights using NumPy and Pandas

The Dataset

We will use the Public School Teachers Salaries dataset from California's fiscal year 2010-2011 made available through data.ca.gov. It contains information on over 250,000 teacher salary records across various metrics like district, county, years experience etc. Dataset link:

https://data.ca.gov/dataset/public-school-teachers-salaries

Note that for this exercise, I have converted the originally ~250MB CSV file into a smaller subset JSON sample you can download here:

https://filebin.net/0x3bkt5hydasgv12

This makes the exercise more manageable while fitting dataset into tutorial flow and compute environments. Feel free to follow along on the full dataset for more significant analysis.

Problem Statement

Our objectives through analyzing this teacher salary data will be:

1. Determine districts with highest average teacher salaries
2. Understand variation is salary by key dimensions like district, experience
3. Surface insights that may help optimize spending

Setup

Let's setup an isolated Python environment and install packages:

```
code
$ python3 -m venv analyze_salaries

$ source analyze_salaries/bin/activate

$ pip install numpy pandas jupyter
```

Jupyter Notebook enables interactive analysis complementary to scripts we will leverage.

Download the sample salaries data JSON from link above into the environment folder.

Launch a Jupyter notebook with:

```
code
$ jupyter notebook
We are ready to start analysis!
** Data Loading and Inspection **
```

First, import our core packages - NumPy and Pandas:

```
python
```

```
code
import numpy as np
import pandas as pd
```

Load the salaries JSON exported from SQLite database:

```
python
code
df = pd.read_json('salaries.json')
```

Check top few records with .head():

```
python
code
df.head()

#or print full dataframe
print(df)
```

This shows various dimensions around teacher compensation like district name, years of experience as well as actual salary paid across years.

Next, let's check out dataframe shape - number of rows and columns along with data types and null values per column:

```
python
code
df.info()
```

gives overview of 17 columns spanning basic metadata, district details and financials. No nulls implies clean complete dataset.

Inspecting distributions of key numeric columns will help analysis:

```
python
code
print(df['Average Salary'].describe())
```

```
print(df['Years Experience'].describe())
```

Statistics like mean and percentiles on these fields provide useful context.

Data Cleansing

With initial inspection done, we prepare the data for analysis by handling anomalies like missing values, formatting issues etc.

First we fill any null 'Average Salary' values to ensure computations work properly in analysis stage:

```
python
 code
avg_salary_mean = df['Average Salary'].mean()


df['Average Salary'] = df['Average Salary'].
fillna(avg_salary_mean)
```

Next we format 'District Name' to title case for consistency:

```
python
 code
df['District Name'] = df['District Name'].str.title()
```

Finally we take subset of columns relevant for analysis goals keeping data tidy:

```
python
 code
df = df[['District Name', 'County Name',
         'Years Experience', 'Average Salary']]
```

We now have a clean view focussing on key dimensions.

Exploratory Analysis

With data ready, we probe, visualize and question the data for insights...

To start, which California counties pay teachers the highest on average?

```
python
 code
df.groupby('County Name').agg({'Average Salary':
'mean'}) \
            .sort_values('Average Salary',
ascending=False) \
            .reset_index(name='Avg Salary')
# Or just:
df.groupby('County')['Average Salary'].mean().sort_
values(ascending=False)
```

We see counties like Los Angeles, Alameda and Santa Clara lead average compensation. Interesting to explore this county level variation.

How does average salary vary by years of teacher experience?

```
python
 code
df.groupby('Years Experience').agg({'Average Salary':
'mean'}) \
           .sort_values('Average Salary') \
           .reset_index(name='Avg Salary')
```

We note average salary positively correlates to years of experience indicating higher pay for seasoned teachers.

What are the top 10 highest paying school districts irrespective of years experience?

```
python
 code
df.groupby('District Name')['Average Salary'] \
```

```
    .mean() \
    .sort_values(ascending=False) \
    .head(10)
```

Here we spot outliers with very high average pay. Granular district analysis reveals opportunities.

Cross filtering on multiple dimensions helps deeper analysis...

Do teachers with 10-15 years of experience get paid more in San Francisco county compared to state average for similar experience?

```
python
 code
sf = df[(df['Years Experience']>=10) &
        (df['Years Experience']<=15) &
        (df['County Name']=='San Francisco')]

state_avg = df[(df['Years Experience']>=10) &
               (df['Years Experience']<=15)]
['Average Salary'].mean()

print(f'San Francisco County: {round(sf["Average
Salary"].mean(), 2)}')
print(f'California State Average: {round(state_avg,
2)}')
```

We see San Francisco does pay its mid-senior band teachers 10% higher than state benchmarks. Many such dual segmentation analyses reveal geo, experience and district strategy comparisons.

There are dozens more experiments we could devise leveraging NumPy and Pandas on this salaries dataset for a thorough compensation analysis!

Key Takeaways

In this exercise we explored essential Python data analysis tools on real world salary data for the following insights:

1. Significant variation in average teacher compensation across California counties

2. Strong positive correlation of average salary to years of teaching experience

3. School districts with exceptionally high average pay warranting deeper evaluation

4. Multi-dimensional filtering and grouping enabling apples-to-apples comparisons

The workflow demonstrates a repeatable template useful for other analysis needs - scoped problem, thorough data inspection, cleansing and standardization followed by creative empirical interrogation with Python.

NumPy enabled efficient multi-dimensional analytics while Pandas provided versatile data manipulation capabilities making analysis intuitive.

There are many directions analysis could be taken further on this data. Additional visualizations with Matplotlib would make insights more communicative. Scraping or loading complementary datasets - population, income levels, student teacher ratios etc per region and district could give further context. Predictive analytics around optimal compensation is another avenue with salary used as target variable for modeling.

Chapter 2: Working with APIs

Technology is all around us in the modern world, and practically everything is linked together via the internet. We keep in touch with those we care about, explore the internet, and carry out a variety of chores by using a variety of programs that are available on our mobile devices and personal computers. Under the scenes, these apps make use of application programming interfaces (APIs) to connect to a variety of services and get data that is necessary to carry out certain activities.

In this chapter, we will talk about application programming interfaces (APIs), HTTP requests, the JSON data format, and using Python to access APIs. We will also go through several prominent application programming interfaces (APIs) that may be used to get data from a variety of services.

What are APIs?

The acronym "API" stands for "Application Programming Interface," and it refers to a collection of guidelines that specifies how various software programs may communicate with one another. To put it more simply, it is a bridge that enables several programs to communicate with one another and exchange information as well as services.

There are several varieties of application programming interfaces (APIs), including Web APIs, Local APIs, Cloud APIs, and more. The most common kind of application programming interface (API) is called a web API, and it gives us access to a variety of online-based services like X (Twitter), Facebook, Google Maps, and many more.

Types of APIs

The following are some of the many kinds of APIs:

- RESTful APIs: RESTful APIs are application programming interfaces that adhere to the Representational State Transfer (REST) architectural principles while developing web services. Web services and mobile apps make extensive use of RESTful application programming interfaces (APIs), which are intended to be user-friendly, scalable, and adaptable in nature.
- SOAP APIs, which stands for Simple Object Access Protocol, is a data exchange protocol between applications that uses structured data. SOAP APIs are commonly used for corporate applications due to their increased complexity when compared to RESTful APIs.
- GraphQL APIs: GraphQL is a query language for application programming interfaces (APIs) that enables users to describe the data that they want and then get just that data in return. GraphQL was developed by Facebook. Because of their adaptability and capacity to lower overall network load, GraphQL APIs are quickly gaining a significant following.

HTTP Requests and Responses

The term "Hypertext Transfer Protocol" (often known simply as "HTTP") refers to the fundamental protocol that is used while transferring data over the internet. In the context of application programming interfaces (APIs), we utilize HTTP requests to communicate with a particular service in order to get a response.

There are many distinct varieties of HTTP requests, including GET, POST, PUT, and DELETE, among others. Requests with the GET verb are used to get data from a particular service, and requests with the POST verb are used to provide data to that particular service.

When we submit an HTTP request to a particular service, the response that we get back is also in the HTTP format. Several pieces of information, including status codes, headers, and data, are included inside an HTTP response. Although the headers hold details about the response, the status code informs us whether or not the request was successful.

Overview of HTTP protocol

As the Hypertext Transfer Protocol (HTTP) is a stateless protocol, it follows that each request and answer are completely separate from one another and any prior requests or responses. When a client wants to access a certain resource, it will send an HTTP request to the server. This request will comprise a method (like GET or POST) and a URL (Uniform Resource Locator) that will identify the resource. The data that was requested is included in the HTTP response that is subsequently sent back by the server. This response contains a status code (such as 200 for success or 404 for not found).

Sending and receiving HTTP requests with Python

Python comes with a number of libraries that may be used to send and receive HTTP requests. These libraries include the built-in urllib library as well as the Requests library that is provided by a third party. Because of its intuitive design and user-friendliness, the Requests library enjoys widespread use.

JSON Data Format

JSON is an acronym that stands for JavaScript Object Notation. It describes a format for the exchange of data that is lightweight and simple to read and write. It is often used for the purpose of transferring data across several apps since it is based on a subset of the computer language known as JavaScript.

The data in JSON is structured in key-value pairs, and it is very much like a dictionary in Python in this regard. It's capable of holding a variety of data kinds, including texts, integers, booleans, arrays, and objects, among others.

Introduction to JSON

The representation of data in JSON is a collection of key-value pairs, very much like a dictionary in the programming language Python. JSON data is generally used to represent structured data such as user profiles or product listings. JSON data may include nested structures such as arrays and objects, and it can also contain other data types.

Parsing and creating JSON data in Python

Working with JSON data is made easier using Python's built-in support, which is accessed via the json module. The json module includes methods that may be used to create JSON data from Python objects as well as functions that can parse JSON data into Python objects.

JSON (JavaScript Object Notation) has become the predominant data format for web APIs allowing structured data exchange. Its nested structures similar to Python dictionaries/lists can represent complex real world data across various domains:

```
json
 code
{
   "userId": 1,
```

```
    "id": 1,
    "title": "Example",
    "tags": ["tech","code"],
    "stats": {
        "views": 148,
        "likes": 28
    }
}
```

Here single post objects have commenting, tagging and analytics metadata. Such composition accommodates evolving schemas. Lightweight serialization ensures high performance networking. Nearly every modern API returns JSON responses making parsing seamless across languages.

Accessing APIs with Python

Sending HTTP queries and managing the replies to those requests is required when using APIs with Python. To our good fortune, Python has a number of libraries, one of which is called the Requests library, which streamlines the procedure. Python's Requests library is a module that may be used to send HTTP requests to other resources on the internet, such as application programming interfaces (APIs).

Using the Requests library to access APIs

Installing the Requests library is the first step toward putting it to use in your projects. With the Python package installer known as pip, the Requests library may be installed on your computer. Launch the command prompt or terminal on your computer and enter the following command to install the Requests library:

```
pip install requests
```

When the Requests library has been installed on your computer, you can use it to access APIs by making HTTP requests to the endpoints of the

API. GET, POST, PUT, and DELETE are the HTTP request methods that are used the most often. Data may be retrieved from the server using the GET method, while data can be sent to the server using the POST method, existing data can be updated using the PUT method, and data can be deleted using the DELETE method.

Authentication with APIs

Authentication is required to utilize many application programming interfaces (APIs), which ensures that only authorized users may access the data. API keys, OAuth 1.0a, and OAuth 2.0 are some of the several kinds of authentication techniques that may be used by application programming interfaces (APIs).

A straightforward method of authentication, API keys require the submission of a one-of-a-kind key in the form of a parameter inside the API request. The key, which is normally supplied by the API provider, is used in the process of identifying the person who is making the request. The OAuth 1.0a and OAuth 2.0 authentication methods are more complicated than others since they need the client and the server to trade tokens with one another.

If you want to use an API that needs authentication, you will need to include the authentication information in the request that you send. Either by using an Authentication header in the request or by including the authentication information in the request itself as a parameter, this objective may be accomplished.

Python provides easy API integration through its requests module. We will access placeholder API data from JSONPlaceholder demonstrating common workflows:

```
python
 code
import requests
```

```
url = 'https://jsonplaceholder.typicode.com/posts'

response = requests.get(url)
posts = response.json()

print(type(posts)) # List of posts as dicts
print(posts[0]['title']) # Prints post title
```

We send HTTP GET request to URL and access returned list of post objects now converted to native Python data structures. API data becomes available for application logic and workflows.

Requests allows payment of parameters:

```
python
 code
response = requests.get(url,
params={'category':'tech'})
tech_posts = response.json()
Here category filters posts. Requests handles URL
formation, HTTP and serialization abstracting API
complexities.
For creating and updating via POST, PUT methods:
python
 code
post_data = {
   'title': 'New Post',
   'content': 'Post content'
}

response = requests.post(url, json=post_data)
new_post = response.json()
print(new_post['id']) # Prints new post id
```

Requests empowers direct interaction eliminating much boilerplate around consuming APIs in Python or any language.

Examples of Popular APIs

There are a great number of widely used APIs that may be used to get access to a diverse collection of data and services. The following are some examples:

X (Twitter) API

Access to the data and services offered by X (Twitter), such as tweets, timelines, and user profiles, may be gained via the usage of the X (Twitter) API. You may construct personalized X (Twitter) clients with the help of the X (Twitter) API, as well as do data analysis on X (Twitter) and other tasks.

Establishing a X (Twitter) Developer account and acquiring API credentials are prerequisites to using the X (Twitter) Application Programming Interface (API). After you have your API keys, you can submit HTTP queries to the X (Twitter) API endpoints by using the Requests library. These requests will be sent to X (Twitter).

OpenWeatherMap API

The OpenWeatherMap API makes it possible to get weather information for locations all over the globe. You may receive information on the current weather conditions, upcoming predictions, and historical data by using the OpenWeatherMap API.

You are going to need to sign up for an account and get an API key before you can access the OpenWeatherMap API. After you have your API key, you may submit HTTP queries to the OpenWeatherMap API endpoints by using the Requests library. These requests will be sent from your browser.

Google Maps API

The Google Maps Application Programming Interface (API) gives users access to a broad variety of mapping and location-based services, such as geocoding, maps, and directions. You may construct custom maps with the help of the Google Maps API, as well as show location-based information on your website using these capabilities.

You will need to sign up for a Google Cloud Platform account and get an API key before you can use the Google Maps application programming interface (API). After you have your API key, you can make HTTP queries to the Google Maps API endpoints by using the Requests library.

We have covered the fundamentals of application programming interfaces (APIs) and how to make use of them with Python in this chapter. We have discussed a variety of subjects, including HTTP requests and replies, the JSON data structure, using APIs with Python, authenticating with APIs, and prominent APIs as examples.

If you are able to grasp the strategies and ideas presented in this chapter, you will be able to begin developing your own apps that make use of the power provided by APIs. You are able to extend your apps and give users with additional functionality by accessing a variety of data and services thanks to the broad number of application programming interfaces (APIs) that are accessible.

Exercises

Exercise 1: Import requests package

Exercise 2: Make GET API call to JSONPlaceholder /posts endpoint to fetch sample data

Exercise 3: Use new post data: {"title": "My New Post", "body": "Content here"} to make POST request creating a new resource.

Chapter 3: Data Analysis and Visualization

Data analysis and visualization are critical components of many industries today, including finance, healthcare, and marketing. Python's popularity for data analysis can be attributed to its wide range of libraries such as Pandas, Matplotlib, and Seaborn. This chapter will delve into the different aspects of data analysis and visualization with Python.

Reading Data with Pandas

Pandas is a popular library in Python for data analysis. It provides various functionalities, including the capability to read and manipulate various types of data. Pandas offers several functions to read data from different sources such as CSV files, Excel files, SQL databases, and more.

For example, to read a CSV file in Pandas, we can use the read_csv() function. This function accepts several parameters, such as the file path, delimiter, header, and column names. For example, if we have a CSV file named data.csv with the following content:

```
id,name,age
1,John,25
2,Jane,30
3,Bob,40
```

We can read it into a Pandas DataFrame by running the following code:

```
import pandas as pd

df = pd.read_csv('data.csv')
print(df)
```

This will produce the following output:

```
   id  name  age
0   1  John   25
1   2  Jane   30
2   3   Bob   40
```

Similarly, we can read Excel files using the read_excel() function, which accepts the file path, sheet name, and other optional parameters. For instance, if we have an Excel file named data.xlsx with a sheet named Sheet1, we can read it into a DataFrame as follows:

```
import pandas as pd

df = pd.read_excel('data.xlsx', sheet_name='Sheet1')
print(df)
```

This will produce the following output:

```
   id  name  age
0   1  John   25
1   2  Jane   30
```

```
2   3   Bob   40
```

Finally, to read data from a SQL database, we can use the read_sql() function. This function requires a connection to the database, which can be established using a database driver such as psycopg2 for PostgreSQL or mysql-connector-python for MySQL. For example, to read data from a PostgreSQL database, we can run the following code:

```
import pandas as pd
import psycopg2

conn = psycopg2.connect(
    host="localhost",
    database="mydatabase",
    user="myusername",
    password="mypassword"
)

df = pd.read_sql('SELECT * FROM mytable', conn)
print(df)
```

This will produce a DataFrame with the results of the SQL query.

Pandas offers a range of functions to read data from different sources. By using these functions, analysts can easily load data into a Pandas DataFrame and start exploring and analyzing the data using the library's powerful data manipulation and analysis tools.

Importing data into Pandas

To import data into Pandas, we can use functions like read_csv(), read_excel(), and read_sql(). For example, to read a CSV file, we can use the read_csv() function:

import pandas as pddata = pd.read_csv('data.csv')

Working with different data formats

Pandas can handle various data formats, including CSV, Excel, SQL, JSON, and more. We can use the appropriate Pandas function to read data from different formats. For example, to read an Excel file, we can use the read_excel() function:

```
import pandas as pddata = pd.read_excel('data.xlsx')
```

Data Cleaning and Preparation

Data cleaning and preparation are essential steps in any data analysis project. In Python, there are several tools and libraries that can be used to perform these tasks efficiently.

Data cleaning involves identifying and correcting errors, inconsistencies, and inaccuracies in the data. This can include removing missing or duplicate values, handling outliers, and transforming data into a more suitable format. Data preparation involves transforming and restructuring the data to prepare it for analysis, such as normalizing or scaling data, or creating new features.

One commonly used library in Python for data cleaning and preparation is Pandas. Pandas provides a variety of functions for handling missing data, removing duplicates, and performing basic data transformations. For example, the dropna() function can be used to remove any rows or columns that contain missing data, while the fillna() function can be used to replace missing values with a specified value or method, such as the mean or median.

Pandas also provides a range of tools for data manipulation, such as merging and joining datasets, grouping data by specific criteria, and reshaping data using pivot tables. These functions can be used to transform data into a more suitable format for analysis.

In addition to Pandas, other Python libraries that can be used for data cleaning and preparation include NumPy, Scikit-Learn, and TensorFlow.

NumPy provides functions for numerical analysis, including handling missing values, while Scikit-Learn is a machine learning library that includes preprocessing functions for scaling and normalizing data. TensorFlow is a deep learning library that can be used for more complex data preparation tasks, such as image or text processing.

Data cleaning and preparation are essential steps in any data analysis project, and Python provides a range of libraries and tools for performing these tasks efficiently. By using these tools, analysts can transform raw data into a more suitable format for analysis, and ensure that their results are accurate and reliable.

Handling missing data

Missing data can cause errors in data analysis and visualization. Pandas provides several functions to handle missing data, including fillna(), dropna(), and interpolate(). For example, to replace missing values with the mean of the column, we can use the fillna() function:

```
import pandas as pdimport numpy as npdata = pd.read_csv('data.csv')
data = data.fillna(data.mean())
```

Data normalization and scaling

Data normalization and scaling involve transforming data into a standard format to ensure fair comparison between variables. Pandas provides several functions to normalize and scale data, including StandardScaler(), MinMaxScaler(), and RobustScaler(). For example, to normalize the data using the MinMaxScaler, we can use the following code:

```
import pandas as pdfrom sklearn.preprocessing import MinMaxScalerdata = pd.read_csv('data.csv')scaler = MinMaxScaler()data_normalized = scaler.fit_transform(data)
```

Exploratory Data Analysis

Exploratory Data Analysis (EDA) is a crucial step in understanding and summarizing the main characteristics of a dataset. This process includes using statistical and visualization techniques to gain insights into the data, identify patterns, and detect anomalies. Python offers various libraries that can be used for EDA, including Matplotlib, Pandas, Seaborn, and Plotly.

The first step in EDA is to load the data into a Pandas DataFrame, as discussed in the previous answer. Once the data is loaded, we can use various functions to get an overview of the data, such as head() and tail() to see the first and last rows of the data, info() to get information about the data types and number of non-null values in each column, and describe() to get a summary of the numerical columns.

After getting an overview of the data, we can start exploring it in more detail using visualization techniques. Matplotlib and Seaborn are two popular Python libraries for creating various types of plots, such as histograms, scatter plots, box plots, and heatmaps. These plots can help us identify patterns and relationships between variables, detect outliers and anomalies, and get a better understanding of the distribution of the data.

For example, we can create a scatter plot to visualize the relationship between two numerical variables, or a histogram to see the distribution of a single variable. We can also use box plots to compare the distribution of a variable across different categories, such as the distribution of ages for males and females.

Apart from visualization, statistical techniques can be utilized to investigate data as well. For example, we can compute summary statistics such as average, median, and standard deviation to acquire more insights into the central tendency and dispersion of the data. Correlation coefficients can also be calculated to assess the intensity and direction of the relationship between two variables.

EDA can also involve identifying and handling missing or incorrect data, dealing with outliers, and transforming the data to prepare it for analysis.

These tasks can be done using various functions and techniques provided by Pandas and other libraries.

Exploratory Data Analysis (EDA) is a crucial step in any data analysis project. By using various techniques and tools in Python, we can gain insights into the data, identify patterns, and detect anomalies. This can help us make informed decisions about how to proceed with the data analysis and prepare the data for modeling and prediction.

Summary statistics and visualizations

Summary statistics provide a quick and easy way to understand the data and identify any patterns or trends. Pandas provides several functions to compute summary statistics, including describe(), mean(), median(), and more. We can also use visualizations to summarize the data and identify patterns or trends. Matplotlib and Seaborn are popular Python libraries for creating visualizations.

Data profiling and exploration techniques

Data profiling involves examining the data in detail to understand its structure, relationships, and patterns. We can use techniques like scatter plots, box plots, histograms, and more to explore the data in detail. Pandas and Seaborn provide several functions for data profiling and exploration, including pairplot(), scatterplot(), boxplot(), and more.

Visualizing Data with Matplotlib and Seaborn

Data visualization is a key aspect of data analysis and communication. In Python, Matplotlib and Seaborn are two powerful libraries for creating various types of plots and visualizations.

Matplotlib is a plotting library that offers extensive customization options and supports a variety of plot types, including line plots, scatter plots, bar plots, and histograms. To create a plot in Matplotlib, we need to create a figure object and one or more axes objects. Once we have created the axes object, we can use its various methods to add data and customize the plot. For instance, we can use the plot() method to generate a line plot or the scatter() method to produce a scatter plot.

Here is an example of creating a simple line plot using Matplotlib:

```
import matplotlib.pyplot as plt
import numpy as np

x = np.arange(0, 10, 0.1)
y = np.sin(x)

fig, ax = plt.subplots()
ax.plot(x, y)
ax.set_xlabel('x')
ax.set_ylabel('y')
ax.set_title('Sin(x) Plot')

plt.show()
```

This will create a plot of the sine function.

Seaborn is a higher-level plotting library that provides a more streamlined interface and a set of pre-defined styles and color palettes. Seaborn is a higher-level data visualization library that is built on top of Matplotlib. It provides an easy-to-use interface for creating various types of plots, such as scatter plots, line plots, heatmaps, and box plots, with visually appealing styles and color palettes. With Seaborn, complex plots can be created with just a few lines of code.

Here is an example of creating a scatter plot using Seaborn

```
import seaborn as sns
import pandas as pd
```

```
df = pd.read_csv('data.csv')
sns.scatterplot(x='x', y='y', data=df)
```

This will create a scatter plot of the x and y variables in the DataFrame df.

In addition to creating basic plots, both Matplotlib and Seaborn offer a wide range of customization options to fine-tune the appearance of the plot. For example, we can add legends, titles, and axis labels, change the color and size of the data points, and adjust the layout and spacing of the plot.

Matplotlib and Seaborn are powerful libraries for creating various types of plots and visualizations in Python. By using these libraries, we can effectively communicate insights and patterns in the data to others, and make informed decisions based on the analysis.

Creating charts and graphs with Matplotlib

Matplotlib provides a wide range of customization options for creating different types of charts and graphs. The library allows users to create simple line plots, scatter plots, and bar charts using just a few lines of code. Matplotlib also provides advanced customization options for adding titles, labels, legends, and annotations to the charts.

Using Seaborn for advanced visualization

Seaborn is built on top of Matplotlib and provides more advanced visualizations with built-in themes. The library provides support for creating more complex visualizations like heatmaps, cluster plots, violin plots, and pair plots. Seaborn also provides options for customizing the visualizations with different color palettes and themes.

Basic Statistical Analysis with Python

Statistical analysis is an important aspect of data analysis, as it helps us understand the characteristics of the data and make informed decisions based on the analysis. In Python, there are several libraries that can be used for statistical analysis, such as NumPy, Pandas, and SciPy. In this answer, we will cover basic statistical analysis techniques in Python, including descriptive statistics and hypothesis testing.

Descriptive Statistics

Descriptive statistics is the process of summarizing and describing the main characteristics of a dataset. This includes measures of central tendency, such as the mean, median, and mode, and measures of variability, such as the standard deviation, variance, and range. In Python, we can use NumPy and Pandas to calculate these descriptive statistics.

Here is an example of calculating the mean, median, and standard deviation of a dataset using NumPy:

```
import numpy as np


data = np.array([1, 2, 3, 4, 5])
mean = np.mean(data)
median = np.median(data)
std = np.std(data)


print("Mean:", mean)
print("Median:", median)
print("Standard Deviation:", std)
```

This will output the mean, median, and standard deviation of the dataset.

We can also use Pandas to calculate descriptive statistics for a DataFrame. For example, we can use the describe() method to get a summary of the numerical columns:

```
import pandas as pd
```

```
df = pd.read_csv('data.csv')
print(df.describe())
```

This will output a summary of the numerical columns in the DataFrame, including the count, mean, standard deviation, and quartiles.

Hypothesis Testing

Hypothesis testing is a statistical method used to determine the validity of a hypothesis regarding a population parameter. The process entails establishing both a null hypothesis and an alternative hypothesis, selecting a significance level, and computing a test statistic based on the available data. In Python, we can use the SciPy library to perform hypothesis testing.

Here is an example of performing a t-test in SciPy:

```
from scipy.stats import ttest_ind

group1 = [1, 2, 3, 4, 5]
group2 = [6, 7, 8, 9, 10]

stat, p = ttest_ind(group1, group2)
print("Test Statistic:", stat)
print("p-value:", p)
```

This will perform a two-sample t-test on the two groups of data and output the test statistic and p-value. When performing hypothesis testing, the p-value indicates the probability of observing a test statistic as extreme or more extreme than the calculated one, assuming the null hypothesis is true. When the p-value is less than the significance level (typically 0.05), the null hypothesis can be rejected and the alternative hypothesis accepted. Python offers robust libraries for conducting fundamental statistical analysis, including hypothesis testing and descriptive statistics. By utilizing these methods, we can acquire valuable insights from the data and make informed decisions. However, it is important to remember that statistical analysis is only one aspect of data analysis, and should be combined with other techniques such as data cleaning, data visualization, and machine learning to get a complete understanding of the data.

Data analysis and visualization are essential skills for individuals working with data. Python offers a plethora of tools and libraries for data analysis and visualization, such as NumPy, Pandas, Matplotlib, Seaborn, Statsmodels, and SciPy. By learning how to use these tools effectively, you can gain insights from complex data and communicate your findings to others.

Exercises

Exercise 1: Load a CSV dataset into a Pandas DataFrame

Exercise 2: Use .info(), .describe() and .head() to inspect the data

Exercise 3: Handle missing values and formatting issues to clean data

Exercise 4: Find top 5 highest performing products by sales

Exercise 5: Train linear regression model predicting house prices

Exercise 6: Create interactive scatter plot visualization

Chapter 4: Machine Learning with Python

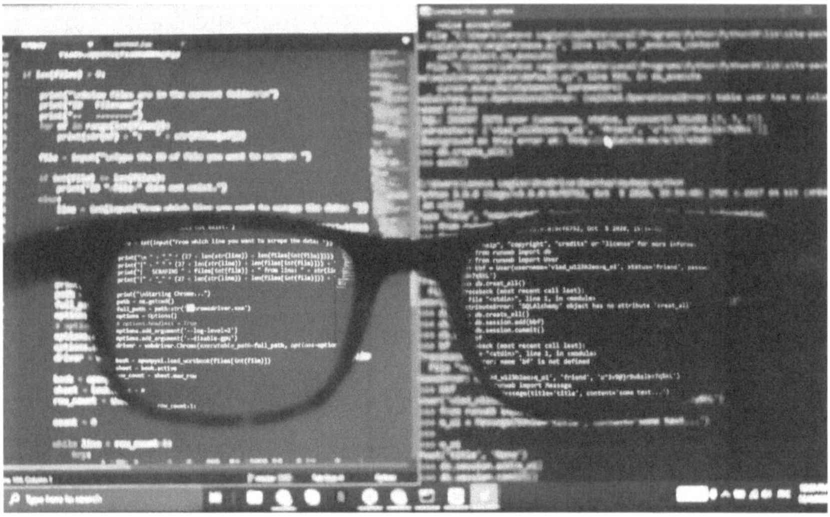

Machine learning is a rapidly growing field that has gained immense popularity over the years. Machine learning is a field of artificial intelligence that focuses on developing algorithms and models that enable machines to learn and make decisions without being explicitly programmed. This article will provide a summary of machine learning concepts and various machine learning algorithms that are utilized in Python.

Overview of Machine Learning

Machine learning refers to the process of training computers to learn from data and use that knowledge to make predictions or decisions. The goal is to create models that can learn from data and apply that learning to new, previously unseen data. Rather than being explicitly programmed, machine learning is a type of artificial intelligence that enables computers to learn from experience.

The main aim of machine learning is to build models that can leverage data to make predictions or decisions. These models rely on algorithms that are developed to learn from data and optimize their performance over time. Machine learning models can be used for a variety of purposes, such as classification, regression, clustering, and recommendation.

Types of Machine Learning Algorithms

A wide variety of machine learning algorithms exist, each with unique advantages and drawbacks. Linear regression, logistic regression, decision trees, random forests, and k-means clustering are among the most commonly used algorithms.

Supervised and Unsupervised Learning

Supervised and unsupervised learning are two fundamental paradigms of machine learning that are used to solve a variety of problems. Both approaches involve learning from data, but they differ in how the data is labeled or unlabeled, and how the learning process takes place. In this answer, we will discuss the difference between supervised and unsupervised learning, as well as provide examples of common algorithms used in each approach.

Supervised Learning

Supervised learning is a machine learning approach that involves learning from data that has been labeled. In this type of learning, a machine is provided with input examples, along with corresponding output labels or target values. The aim is to develop a model that can predict the output label or target value for new input examples. The typical steps involved in supervised learning are as follows:

- Data acquisition: Gathering a set of annotated examples.

- Data preprocessing: Cleaning, standardizing, and modifying the input features and output labels.
- Model selection: Choosing an appropriate machine learning algorithm that is suitable for the specific task.
- Model training: Training the model on the annotated data.
- Evaluation: Assessing the performance of the model on a separate set of annotated data.
- Deployment: Introducing the model into a production environment for predictions on new and unseen data.

Examples of supervised learning algorithms are:

- Linear regression: A regression algorithm that learns a linear function to forecast a continuous output value.
- Logistic regression: A classification algorithm that learns a linear function to forecast a binary or multi-class output label.
- Decision trees: A tree-based algorithm that learns a set of rules to predict a categorical output label.
- Random forests: An ensemble algorithm that combines numerous decision trees to improve prediction accuracy.
- Support vector machines: A classification algorithm that learns a linear or nonlinear function to segregate input examples into distinct categories.
- Neural networks: A group of algorithms that can learn complex nonlinear functions by using multiple interconnected layers of neurons.

Unsupervised Learning

Unsupervised learning is a type of machine learning that involves learning from unlabeled data. In unsupervised learning, the machine is given a set of input examples without any corresponding output labels or target values. The goal is to learn the underlying structure or patterns in the data.

The process of unsupervised learning typically involves the following steps:

Data collection: Collect a set of unlabeled examples.

- Data preparation: Preprocess the data by cleaning, normalizing, and transforming the input features.
- Model selection: Select an appropriate machine learning algorithm that is suitable for the task at hand.
- Training: Train the model on the unlabeled data.
- Evaluation: Evaluate the model's performance by measuring the quality of the learned structure or patterns.
- Deployment: Deploy the model in a production environment to use the learned structure or patterns for various tasks.

Examples of unsupervised learning algorithms include:

- Clustering: A group of algorithms that learn to group similar input examples into clusters or segments based on their similarity.
- Principal component analysis: A dimensionality reduction algorithm that learns to reduce the number of input features while preserving the most important information.
- t-SNE: A dimensionality reduction algorithm that learns to visualize high-dimensional data in a lower-dimensional space.
- Autoencoders: A class of algorithms that can learn to compress and decompress input data by using an encoder and decoder architecture.

- Generative adversarial networks: A class of algorithms that can learn to generate new data by using a generator and discriminator architecture.

Difference between Supervised and Unsupervised Learning

The fundamental difference between supervised and unsupervised learning lies in the presence or absence of labeled data. In supervised learning, labeled data is provided to the machine for learning, while in unsupervised learning, the machine is given unlabeled data to learn from.

Supervised learning is typically used when the task is to predict a certain output label or target value based on input features. For example, predicting whether an email is spam or not based on the text content, or predicting the price of a house based on its location, size, and other features.

On the other hand, unsupervised learning is typically used when the task is to discover hidden patterns or structure in the data. For example, identifying groups of customers with similar buying habits, or identifying anomalies in a dataset that may indicate fraud or errors.

Another key difference between supervised and unsupervised learning is the evaluation metric used to measure the model's performance. In supervised learning, the evaluation is typically based on the accuracy or error rate of the predicted output labels or target values. In unsupervised learning, the evaluation is typically based on the quality of the learned structure or patterns, which may be subjective and difficult to measure.

Finally, it is worth noting that some machine learning tasks may involve both supervised and unsupervised learning. For example, semi-supervised learning involves learning from a combination of labeled and unlabeled data, while reinforcement learning involves learning through trial and error feedback from the environment.

Supervised and unsupervised learning are two fundamental types of machine learning that are used to solve a variety of problems. Supervised learning involves learning from labeled data to predict output labels or target values, while unsupervised learning involves learning from unlabeled data to discover hidden patterns or structure. Both approaches involve selecting an appropriate machine learning algorithm, training the model on the data, evaluating its performance, and deploying it in a production environment. By understanding the difference between supervised and unsupervised learning, we can choose the most appropriate approach for our specific task and improve the accuracy and effectiveness of our machine learning models.

Scikit-Learn Library

Scikit-Learn is built on top of NumPy, SciPy, and Matplotlib, which are other popular libraries for scientific computing in Python. It has a consistent API and follows the principles of object-oriented programming, making it easy to use and extend. Scikit-Learn also provides a range of tools for data preprocessing, model evaluation, and model tuning, which help to streamline the machine learning workflow.

Using Scikit-Learn for machine learning tasks

To use Scikit-Learn for a machine learning task, we first need to load the data into a suitable format. Scikit-Learn accepts data in the form of NumPy arrays, Pandas dataframes, or SciPy sparse matrices. We then split the data into training and test sets using the train_test_split function. The training set is used to train the machine learning model, while the test set is used to evaluate its performance.

Once we have split the data, we can select an appropriate machine learning algorithm for the task at hand. Scikit-Learn provides a wide range of algorithms, each with its own strengths and weaknesses. For example, we can use logistic regression for binary classification tasks, decision trees for multi-class classification tasks, and linear regression for regression tasks.

After selecting the algorithm, we can instantiate the model and fit it to the training data using the fit method. This step involves learning the model parameters from the training data. Once the model is trained, we can use it to make predictions on new data using the predict method.

To evaluate the performance of the model, we can use a range of metrics such as accuracy, precision, recall, F1 score, and AUC-ROC score. Scikit-Learn provides functions for computing these metrics, as well as tools for visualizing the results using Matplotlib.

In addition to basic machine learning tasks, Scikit-Learn provides a range of tools for data preprocessing and feature extraction. For example, we can use the StandardScaler function to normalize the data, the OneHotEncoder function to encode categorical variables, and the PCA function to perform dimensionality reduction. Scikit-Learn also provides tools for model selection and tuning, such as cross-validation and grid search, which help to optimize the model hyperparameters and improve its performance.

Examples of using Scikit-Learn for machine learning tasks

Here are some examples of using Scikit-Learn for common machine learning tasks:

- Binary classification: we may want to predict if a customer will purchase a product based on their age, income, and other factors. Using Scikit-Learn's logistic regression, we can create a binary classification model. We begin by loading the data into a Pandas dataframe, then splitting it into training and testing sets. Next, we create the logistic regression model by instantiating the LogisticRegression class and fit it to the training data using the fit method. To evaluate the model, we use metrics like accuracy, precision, and recall to assess its performance.
- Multi-class classification: we might need to classify images of handwritten digits into one of ten possible classes (0-9). To achieve this, we can use Scikit-Learn's decision trees. We start by loading the data into a NumPy array and splitting it into training and testing sets. We then instantiate the decision tree model using the

DecisionTreeClassifier class and fit it to the training data using the fit method. Finally, we evaluate the model performance using metrics such as accuracy, precision, and recall.

- Regression: suppose we want to predict the price of a new house based on its location, size, and other features. Scikit-Learn's linear regression can help us build a regression model. We load the data into a Pandas dataframe, split it into training and testing sets, and instantiate the linear regression model using the LinearRegression class. We fit the model to the training data using the fit method and make predictions on the test data using the predict method. Finally, we evaluate the model's performance using metrics such as mean squared error and R-squared.
- Clustering: Suppose we have a dataset of customer purchasing behavior and we want to identify groups of customers with similar purchasing patterns. We can use k-means clustering from Scikit-Learn to cluster the customers. We first load the data into a NumPy array, normalize it using the StandardScaler function, and then instantiate the k-means clustering model using the KMeans class. We then fit the model to the data using the fit method and assign each customer to a cluster using the predict method. Finally, we can visualize the results using Matplotlib.

Scikit-Learn is a powerful and easy-to-use library for machine learning in Python. It provides a wide range of supervised and unsupervised learning algorithms, as well as tools for data preprocessing, model evaluation, and model tuning. By using Scikit-Learn, we can quickly and easily build machine learning models for a variety of tasks, from binary classification to clustering.

Common Machine Learning Algorithms

Machine learning algorithms are at the core of the field of machine learning. These algorithms are used to build models that can learn from data and make predictions on new, unseen data. There are many different machine learning algorithms, each with its strengths and weaknesses, and it is important for a data scientist to be familiar with a wide range of algorithms to choose the best one for a given problem. In this article, we will discuss some of the most common machine learning algorithms.

1. Linear Regression: Linear regression is a statistical method that is used to establish a relationship between two or more variables. It is a type of supervised learning algorithm where the input variables (also known as independent variables) are used to predict the output variable (also known as the dependent variable). The goal of linear regression is to find the line of best fit that can explain the relationship between the input variables and the output variable. The line of best fit is a straight line that minimizes the sum of the squared differences between the predicted and actual values. Linear regression is used in many applications, such as predicting housing prices, stock prices, and customer lifetime value.

2. Logistic Regression: Logistic regression is a type of supervised learning algorithm used for binary classification problems. It is used to predict the probability of a binary output variable (also known as the dependent variable) based on one or more input variables (also known as the independent variables). The goal of logistic regression is to find the relationship between the input variables and the probability of the output variable being true (i.e., having a value of 1). Logistic regression is widely used in various applications, such as predicting whether a patient will develop a disease or not, or whether an email is spam or not.

3. Decision Trees: Decision trees are a supervised learning algorithm used for classification and regression tasks. They recursively divide the data into smaller subsets based on the input variable values. Each internal node represents a decision based on an input variable, and each leaf node represents a prediction or classification based on the decision path. Decision trees are useful for various applications, such as predicting customer purchasing behavior based on demographic and purchase history.

4. Random Forests: Random forests are an ensemble learning method that combines multiple decision trees to improve performance and reduce overfitting. They train multiple decision trees on different data and input variable subsets. The final prediction is based on the predictions of all decision trees. Random forests are useful for applications like predicting customer churn or detecting fraudulent transactions.

5. K-means Clustering: K-means clustering is an unsupervised learning algorithm that clusters data into groups based on similarity. It randomly selects k centroids and assigns each data point to the nearest centroid using a distance metric. The centroids are then updated based on the mean of the assigned data points, and the process repeats until convergence. K-means clustering is useful for applications such as customer segmentation or image segmentation.

There are many other algorithms and techniques that can be used for different types of problems. It's crucial for data scientists to understand the strengths and weaknesses of each algorithm and select the best one for the problem at hand. It's also often helpful to try multiple algorithms and compare their performance to choose the best one.

Applications of Machine Learning in Python

Machine learning has become a ubiquitous technology in recent years, impacting almost every aspect of our lives. The potential uses of machine learning are vast, spanning from medical diagnosis to customer recommendations. Python is a popular language for implementing machine learning applications, thanks to its simplicity, flexibility, and feature-rich libraries such as Scikit-Learn, TensorFlow, and PyTorch. This article explores some of the most common machine learning applications in Python:

- Image classification: This involves assigning labels to images based on their content, and is used in many applications including face recognition, autonomous vehicles, and medical diagnosis.

Convolutional neural networks (CNNs) are a popular type of neural network used for image classification, and can automatically learn to extract meaningful features from images to classify them into different categories. TensorFlow and Keras offer powerful tools for building and training CNNs for image classification.

- Convolutional neural networks (CNNs) are a widely used type of neural network in image classification tasks. They can automatically extract significant features from images and classify them into different categories. TensorFlow and Keras are two powerful libraries that provide a range of tools for building and training CNNs for image classification.
- Natural language processing (NLP) is a field of machine learning that deals with processing human language. It has applications in various areas such as sentiment analysis, text classification, and machine translation. Python has several powerful libraries for NLP, including NLTK, spaCy, and Gensim, which offer tools for text preprocessing, feature extraction, and building machine learning models for NLP tasks.

Recurrent neural networks (RNNs) are a type of neural network that is commonly used in NLP tasks. They can learn from sequences of input data, making them particularly useful for applications such as language translation and speech recognition.

RNNs can handle variable-length sequences of data and are capable of modeling the dependencies between elements in a sequence. RNNs can process sequences of words or characters and capture the context and meaning of the text. Libraries like TensorFlow and PyTorch provide tools for building and training RNNs for NLP tasks.

- Recommender systems: Recommender systems are used to recommend products or services to users based on their past behavior or preferences. For example, Amazon's product recommendation system recommends products to users based on their browsing and purchase history.

Recommender systems are built using machine learning algorithms that can learn from user behavior and recommend products or services that are likely to be of interest to the user. Collaborative filtering is a popular technique used for building recommender systems. It involves analyzing user behavior and recommending products or services that are similar to those liked by other users.

Python provides a number of powerful libraries for building recommender systems, such as Surprise, LightFM, and TensorFlow Recommenders. These libraries provide tools for building collaborative filtering models and evaluating their performance.

In addition to these three applications, machine learning is used in many other fields such as fraud detection, customer segmentation, and predictive maintenance. Python's simplicity, flexibility, and powerful libraries make it an ideal language for building machine learning applications.

Machine learning is a rapidly growing field that has found applications in various industries. Python's flexibility and the availability of powerful machine learning libraries have made it the preferred choice of data scientists and machine learning engineers. In this chapter, we have discussed some of the popular machine learning algorithms and applications of machine learning in Python. By learning and mastering these concepts and tools, you can build powerful machine learning models and solve complex problems in various domains.

Sample Code Snippets

To illustrate the applications of machine learning in Python as described, I'll provide sample code snippets for some key areas: image classification using a convolutional neural network (CNN) with TensorFlow, natural language processing (NLP) using a recurrent neural network (RNN) with TensorFlow, and a simple example of a recommender system using Python's Surprise library.

1. Image Classification with CNN in TensorFlow

python

```
import tensorflow as tf
from tensorflow.keras import layers, models

# Define a simple CNN model
model = models.Sequential([
    layers.Conv2D(32, (3, 3), activation='relu',
input_shape=(28, 28, 1)),
    layers.MaxPooling2D((2, 2)),
    layers.Conv2D(64, (3, 3), activation='relu'),
    layers.MaxPooling2D((2, 2)),
    layers.Conv2D(64, (3, 3), activation='relu'),
    layers.Flatten(),
    layers.Dense(64, activation='relu'),
    layers.Dense(10, activation='softmax')
])

model.compile(optimizer='adam',
              loss='sparse_categorical_
crossentropy',
              metrics=['accuracy'])

# Assume `train_images`, `train_labels` are your
training data and labels
# model.fit(train_images, train_labels, epochs=5)

model.summary()
```

2. Natural Language Processing (NLP) with RNN in TensorFlow

python

```
import tensorflow as tf

from tensorflow.keras.layers import Embedding,
SimpleRNN, Dense

from tensorflow.keras.models import Sequential


model = Sequential()

model.add(Embedding(10000, 32))

model.add(SimpleRNN(32))

model.add(Dense(1, activation='sigmoid'))


model.compile(optimizer='rmsprop', loss='binary_
crossentropy', metrics=['acc'])


# Assume `input_sequences` and `labels` are your
training data and labels

# model.fit(input_sequences, labels, epochs=10,
batch_size=128)
```

```
model.summary()
```

3. Recommender System with Surprise Library

python

```
from surprise import Dataset, Reader

from surprise import KNNBasic

from surprise.model_selection import train_test_
split

from surprise import accuracy
```

```
# Load your data, assuming `data` is a pandas
DataFrame with user, item, and rating columns
reader = Reader(rating_scale=(1, 5))  # Adjust
rating_scale according to your dataset
data = Dataset.load_from_df(data[['user',
'item', 'rating']], reader)

# Split the dataset for evaluation
trainset, testset = train_test_split(data, test_
size=0.25)

# Use KNNBasic algorithm
algo = KNNBasic()

# Train the algorithm on the trainset, and
predict ratings for the testset
algo.fit(trainset)
predictions = algo.test(testset)

# Compute and print Root Mean Squared Error
accuracy.rmse(predictions)
```

These examples demonstrate foundational approaches to implementing machine learning applications in Python for image classification, natural language processing, and recommender systems. To apply these in real-world projects, you would need to adapt and expand upon these templates, incorporating data preprocessing, model tuning, and possibly more complex model architectures.

Chapter 5: Web Scraping with Python

Web scraping is an effective technique for extracting valuable data from websites. It has become increasingly important as the volume of online data continues to grow. In this section, we will explore the fundamentals of web scraping and how Python can be used to extract data from websites. We will also introduce two popular Python libraries, Requests and BeautifulSoup, and show how to use them for web scraping. Finally, we will discuss how to extract and clean data after scraping.

What is Web Scraping?

Web scraping, sometimes referred to as web harvesting or web data extraction, is the process of automatically collecting data from websites. It involves automated retrieval of information from web pages and transforming it into a structured format that can be used for further analysis. Web scraping can be used to extract a variety of data, including product prices, customer reviews, news articles, social media data, and much more.

Web scraping is an important technique for various applications. For example, in e-commerce, web scraping can be used to collect product prices from various online retailers to help businesses determine competitive pricing. In finance, web scraping can be used to gather news articles and social media sentiment data to make investment decisions. In healthcare, web scraping can be used to collect data from various medical websites for research purposes.

How to Use Python for Web Scraping

Python is an excellent language for web scraping. It has many libraries and tools that make it easy to scrape websites and extract data. In this section, we will discuss some of the popular Python libraries that are used for web scraping.

Requests Library

The Requests library is a Python library that is used to send HTTP requests and handle responses. It makes it easy to interact with web pages and retrieve data from them. The Requests library can be used to send GET and POST requests, handle cookies and sessions, and much more.

To use the Requests library, you first need to install it. You can install it using pip, which is a package manager for Python.

```
pip install requests
```

Once the library is installed, you can import it in your Python code and start using it.

```
import requests
```

BeautifulSoup Library

The BeautifulSoup library is a Python library that is used for parsing HTML and XML documents. It makes it easy to extract data from HTML and XML documents. The BeautifulSoup library can be used to navigate the HTML tree structure, search for specific elements, and extract data from them.

To use the BeautifulSoup library, you first need to install it. You can install it using pip, which is a package manager for Python.

```
pip install beautifulsoup4
```

Once the library is installed, you can import it in your Python code and start using it.

```
from bs4 import BeautifulSoup
```

Scraping Data from Websites

Now that we have discussed the Requests and BeautifulSoup libraries, we can start scraping data from websites. In this section, we will discuss the process of scraping data from a website using Python.

Step 1: Send a GET Request

The first step in scraping data from a website is to send a GET request to the website. The GET request is used to retrieve data from a web page. We can use the Requests library to send a GET request to a website.

```
import requests
url = 'https://example.com'
response = requests.get(url)
print(response.text)
```

In the code above, we send a GET request to https://example.com and store the response in the response variable. We then print the response text using the print() function.

Step 2: Parse the HTML

The second step in scraping data from a website is to parse the HTML. HTML stands for Hypertext Markup Language and is the standard markup language used to create web pages. We can use the BeautifulSoup library to parse the HTML.

```
from bs4 import BeautifulSoup
soup = BeautifulSoup(response.text, 'html.parser')
print(soup.prettify())
```

In the code above, we create a BeautifulSoup object by passing the response text and 'html.parser' to the BeautifulSoup() function. We then print the prettified HTML using the prettify() function.

Step 3: Extract Data

The final step in scraping data from a website is to extract the data that we need. We can use the BeautifulSoup library to extract data from the HTML.

```
from bs4 import BeautifulSoup
soup = BeautifulSoup(response.text, 'html.parser')
title = soup.title
print(title)
first_paragraph = soup.find('p')
print(first_paragraph.text)
```

In the code above, we first create a BeautifulSoup object using the response text. We then extract the title of the page using the title attribute of the soup object. Finally, we extract the text of the first paragraph using the find() method of the soup object.

Data Extraction and Cleaning

After scraping data from a website, we often need to clean and transform the data before using it for further analysis. In this section, we will discuss some techniques for extracting and cleaning data after scraping.

Regular Expressions

Regular expressions, also known as regex, are a powerful tools for pattern matching and text manipulation. They can be used to extract specific patterns from text data. For example, we can use regular expressions to extract email addresses, phone numbers, or dates from text data.

```
import re
text = 'My email address is john@example.com'
email_pattern = r'\b[A-Za-z0-9._%+-]+@
[A-Za-z0-9.-]+\.[A-Z|a-z]{2,}\b'
email = re.search(email_pattern, text)
print(email.group())
```

In the code above, we use the re module to search for an email address in the text variable. We define a regular expression pattern for email addresses and use the search() method of the re module to search for the pattern in the text variable. We then print the email address using the group() method of the search result.

String Manipulation

String manipulation is the process of modifying strings to extract specific data or transform them into a different format. We can use various string manipulation techniques to clean and transform data after scraping.

```
text = 'John Doe (35 years old)'
name = text.split(' ')[0] + ' ' + text.split(' ')[1]
age = text.split(' ')[3].replace('(', '').
replace(')', '')
```

```
print(name)
print(age)
```

In the code above, we use the split() method of the string object to split the text into name and age. We use the replace() method to remove the parentheses around the age. We then print the name and age variables.

Web scraping is a powerful technique for extracting data from websites. Python is an excellent language for web scraping, thanks to its many libraries and tools. In this chapter, we introduced the Requests and BeautifulSoup libraries and showed how to use them for web scraping. We also discussed how to extract and clean data after scraping. With these techniques, you can extract useful data from websites and use it for further analysis.

Practical Exercise - Creating a Simple Web Scraper

In this hands-on exercise, we will build a basic web scraper to extract data from a site using Python. Web scraping is used to collect large amounts of web data for analysis.

We will scrape LinkedIn to gather public profile data helping analyze job trends and professional networking patterns.

Setup

First, we create a dedicated scraper virtual environment:

```
 code
$ python3 -m venv scraper
$ source scraper/bin/activate
$ pip install requests beautifulsoup4 pandas
```

This installs key packages - Requests for making HTTP requests, BeautifulSoup for HTML parsing and Pandas for data analysis.

Making Requests

We will scrape a LinkedIn search URL to get profile results for a query:

```
python
 code
import requests

url = 'https://www.linkedin.com/search/results/
people/?keywords=data%20scientist'
response = requests.get(url)

print(response.status_code) # 200 OK
print(response.headers['Content-Type']) # text/html

html_content = response.text
```

Requests allows issuing GET request returning HTML content to extract data from.

Parsing Content

Next, we leverage BeautifulSoup to parse HTML:

```
python
 code
from bs4 import BeautifulSoup

soup = BeautifulSoup(html_content, 'html.parser')
print(soup.title) # LinkedIn Search | Data Scientist
profiles

# Access meta info, links & data
```

Beautiful lets us navigate the DOM to access elements.

Extracting Data

With search response parsed, we grab key profile data starting with names and job titles:

```
python
 code
profiles = soup.find_all('li', class_='reusable-
search__result-container ')


names = [p.find('span', class_='entity-result__
title').text for p in profiles]


job_titles = [p.find('div', 'entity-result__primary-
subtitle').text for p in profiles]


print(names[:5]) # Print 5 names
print(job_titles[:5]) # Print 5 titles
```

We leverage patterns in page structure to mine attributes. Additional metadata can be extracted through iterating the profiles in similar fashion.

Analysis in Pandas

To enable analysis we store the scraped dataset in a Pandas DataFrame:

```
python
 code
import pandas as pd


data = {'name': names, 'job_title': job_titles}


df = pd.DataFrame(data)
print(df.head())
# Compute stats like common titles, top companies etc
```

There we have a basic web scraper to extract LinkedIn data! The workflow serves as template for expanding scraping efforts. Challenges get more complex handling large batch jobs, authentication, cross-domain requests, detection evasion etc. We will tackle some of these scenarios in the next scraping chapter project.

Chapter 6: Data Science with Python

Introduction to Data Science

Data Science is the field of extracting insights and knowledge from data. It involves the use of various techniques, including statistical analysis, machine learning, data visualization, and data mining, to derive meaningful insights from data. The insights derived from data science can be used to make informed business decisions, improve products and services, and even predict future outcomes.

Data science is a multidisciplinary field that combines elements of statistics, computer science, and domain expertise. The process of data science involves the following steps:

- Defining the problem
- Collecting and preparing the data

- Exploratory data analysis
- Statistical analysis and modeling
- Visualization and communication of results
- Implementation and monitoring

Python is one of the most popular programming languages used in data science due to its simplicity, flexibility, and large community of developers. Python provides several libraries and tools that simplify the process of data analysis, visualization, and modeling.

Working with Data Frames in Python

Data frames are the primary data structure used in data science for manipulating and analyzing data. A data frame is a two-dimensional table-like structure that contains rows and columns of data. Each column in a data frame represents a variable, and each row represents an observation.

Python provides the Pandas library, which is used for data manipulation and analysis. Pandas allows you to read data from various sources, such as CSV, Excel, and SQL databases, and manipulate it using data frames. Data frames can be filtered, sorted, grouped, and transformed using Pandas.

To work with data frames in Python, we primarily use the Pandas library. It allows for easy data manipulation and analysis. Here's a basic example of how to create a data frame, read data from a CSV file, and perform simple operations like filtering and sorting.

```
python
    import pandas as pd


    # Creating a simple data frame
    data = {'Name': ['John', 'Anna', 'Peter',
    'Linda'],
            'Age': [28, 34, 29, 42],
```

```
        'City': ['New York', 'Paris', 'Berlin',
'London']}
df = pd.DataFrame(data)

# Reading data from a CSV file
df_from_csv = pd.read_csv('path/to/your/file.
csv')

# Basic operations
# Filtering
filtered_df = df[df['Age'] > 30]

# Sorting
sorted_df = df.sort_values(by='Age')
```

Data Visualization with Matplotlib and Seaborn

Data visualization is the process of representing data in graphical form to derive insights and communicate results effectively. Python provides two popular libraries for data visualization: Matplotlib and Seaborn.

Matplotlib is a plotting library that allows you to create various types of plots, such as line plots, scatter plots, bar plots, and histograms. Matplotlib provides extensive customization options, such as colors, labels, titles, and legends.

Seaborn is a library that is built on top of Matplotlib and provides a higher-level interface for creating statistical visualizations. Seaborn provides several types of plots, such as heat maps, pair plots, and violin plots. Seaborn also provides various customization options, such as color palettes and themes.

For data visualization, Matplotlib and Seaborn are widely used. Here's how you can create a simple line plot with Matplotlib and a heatmap with Seaborn.

```python
import matplotlib.pyplot as plt
import seaborn as sns
import numpy as np

# Matplotlib line plot
plt.figure(figsize=(10, 6))
plt.plot(df['Age'], label='Age')
plt.title('Simple Line Plot')
plt.xlabel('Index')
plt.ylabel('Age')
plt.legend()
plt.show()

# Seaborn heatmap
data = np.random.rand(4, 6)
sns.heatmap(data, annot=True)
plt.title('Heatmap Example')
plt.show()
```

Exploratory Data Analysis and Statistical Analysis

Exploratory data analysis is the process of analyzing data to summarize its main characteristics, such as its distribution, central tendency, and variability. Exploratory data analysis is an essential step in data science as it helps to identify patterns, outliers, and missing values in the data.

Statistical analysis is the process of applying statistical methods to data to infer relationships and patterns. Statistical analysis involves the use of techniques such as hypothesis testing, regression analysis, and analysis of variance. Statistical analysis is used to answer questions such as whether there is a significant relationship between two variables, whether there is a significant difference between two groups, and whether a model can predict an outcome accurately.

Python provides several libraries for statistical analysis, such as NumPy, SciPy, and Statsmodels. NumPy provides support for mathematical operations on arrays, while SciPy provides statistical functions and algorithms. Statsmodels provides advanced statistical models and methods for data analysis.

Exploratory Data Analysis (EDA) and statistical analysis can be performed using libraries like Pandas, NumPy, and SciPy.

```
python
    import numpy as np
    import pandas as pd
    from scipy import stats

    # Basic EDA with Pandas
    print(df.describe())  # Summary statistics
    print(df['Age'].value_counts())  # Frequency
    counts

    # Statistical Analysis with SciPy
    # T-test example
    t_stat, p_val = stats.ttest_1samp(df['Age'], 30)
    print(f'T-statistic: {t_stat}, P-value: {p_
    val}')
```

Linear and Logistic Regression Analysis

Regression analysis is a statistical technique used to model the relationship between a dependent variable and one or more independent variables. Linear regression is a type of regression analysis that models a linear relationship between the dependent variable and one or more independent variables. Linear regression is used to predict a continuous outcome variable.

Logistic regression is a type of regression analysis that models the relationship between a dependent variable and one or more independent variables. Logistic regression is used to predict a binary outcome variable, such as whether will buy a product or not.

Python provides several libraries for regression analysis, such as Statsmodels and Scikit-learn. Statsmodels provides advanced statistical models for regression analysis, such as generalized linear models and mixed-effects models. Scikit-learn provides machine learning algorithms for regression analysis, such as linear regression, ridge regression, and Lasso regression.

Data science is a crucial field that provides valuable insights and knowledge from data. Python provides several libraries and tools that simplify the process of data analysis, visualization, and modeling. The Pandas library is used for data manipulation and analysis, while Matplotlib and Seaborn are used for data visualization. Exploratory data analysis and statistical analysis are essential steps in data science, and Python provides several libraries for these tasks, such as NumPy, SciPy, and Statsmodels. Regression analysis is a common task in data science, and Python provides several libraries for linear and logistic regression analysis, such as Statsmodels and Scikit-learn.

For regression analysis, we can use libraries such as Statsmodels for more statistical-oriented models, and Scikit-learn for machine learning approaches.

Linear Regression with Scikit-learn

```
python
    from sklearn.model_selection import train_test_
    split
    from sklearn.linear_model import LinearRegression
    from sklearn.metrics import mean_squared_error
```

```
# Assuming 'df' is your DataFrame and 'target'
is your target variable
X = df.drop('target', axis=1)
y = df['target']

X_train, X_test, y_train, y_test = train_test_
split(X, y, test_size=0.2)

model = LinearRegression()
model.fit(X_train, y_train)

predictions = model.predict(X_test)
mse = mean_squared_error(y_test, predictions)
print(f'Mean Squared Error: {mse}')
```

Logistic Regression with Scikit-learn

python

```
from sklearn.linear_model import
LogisticRegression
from sklearn.metrics import accuracy_score

# Assuming 'df' is your DataFrame and 'target'
is your binary target variable
X = df.drop('target', axis=1)
y = df['target']

X_train, X_test, y_train, y_test = train_test_
split(X, y, test_size=0.2, random_state=42)

logreg = LogisticRegression()
```

```
logreg.fit(X_train, y_train)

predictions = logreg.predict(X_test)
accuracy = accuracy_score(y_test, predictions)
print(f'Accuracy: {accuracy}')
```

These examples provide a foundational understanding of how to work with data frames, visualize data, perform exploratory and statistical analysis, and conduct regression analyses in Python. Each of these topics can be expanded with more complex and detailed analyses tailored to specific data science projects.

Overall, Python is an excellent language for data science due to its simplicity, flexibility, and large community of developers. By leveraging the power of Python and its libraries, data scientists can extract valuable insights and knowledge from data to make informed business decisions, improve products and services, and even predict future outcomes.

Chapter 7: Web Development with Python

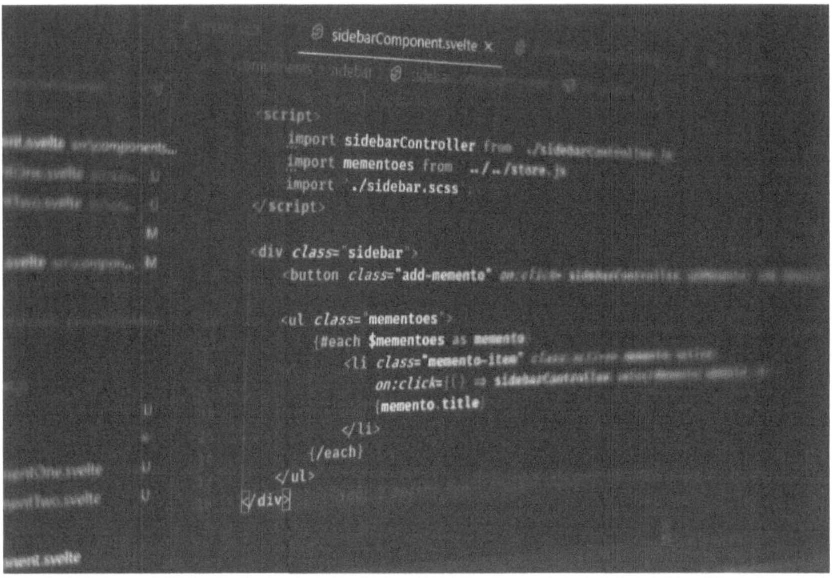

Introduction to Web Development with Python

Web development is the process of creating dynamic websites and web applications. It involves designing, building, and maintaining websites that are accessible to users via the internet. Python is a high-level programming language that can be used for web development. It is easy to learn, versatile, and has a vast library of tools and frameworks.

Python is widely used for web development because of its readability, maintainability, and scalability. Its syntax is simple and easy to understand, making it an ideal language for beginners. Python's large library of tools and frameworks makes it easy to build web applications quickly and efficiently.

Python can be used for both frontend and backend development. For frontend development, Python has various libraries like PyQt, PyGTK, and Kivy. These libraries can be used to create graphical user interfaces (GUIs) and mobile applications. For backend development, Python has web frameworks like Flask, Django, and Pyramid. These frameworks provide a structured way of building web applications and make it easy to handle HTTP requests, routing, and templating.

Python is also widely used for web scraping, which is a technique used for extracting data from websites. Web scraping involves writing code to navigate through a website's HTML structure and extract the required data. Python has several libraries like BeautifulSoup, Scrapy, and Requests-HTML that can be used for web scraping.

Creating Dynamic Websites Using Flask and Django

Flask and Django are two popular web frameworks used for web development with Python. Flask is a micro-framework that is simple, lightweight, and flexible. It is ideal for small to medium-sized web applications that do not require complex functionalities. Flask provides a simple way to handle HTTP requests, routing, and templating. It also has a built-in development server that makes it easy to test the application during development. Flask has a vast library of extensions that can be used to add additional functionalities to the application.

Basic Flask Application

```
python
    from flask import Flask, render_template

    app = Flask(__name__)

    @app.route('/')
    def home():
        return render_template('index.html')
```

```
    if __name__ == '__main__':
        app.run(debug=True)
```

In this example, '***index.html*** 'would be a template file stored in the '***templates'*** directory. Flask uses Jinja2 templating engine, which allows for dynamic content generation in HTML files.

Django, on the other hand, is a full-stack framework that provides everything needed to build complex web applications. It has a robust ORM (Object Relational Mapping) that makes it easy to work with databases. Django provides an admin interface that can be used to manage the application's content. It also has a built-in authentication system that can be used for user management. Django's templating engine is powerful and easy to use, allowing developers to create complex HTML templates easily.

Starting a Django Project

First, install Django using pip and start a project:

```
bash
    pip install django
    django-admin startproject myproject
    cd myproject
```

To create an app within your Django project:

```
bash
    python manage.py startapp myapp
```

Basic Views and URL Configuration in Django

In your app directory (***myapp***), you can define views in ***views.py***:

```
python
    from django.http import HttpResponse
```

```
def home(request):
    return HttpResponse('<h1>Welcome to My Django App</h1>')
```

Then, you need to wire up your views to URLs. In the ***myapp*** directory, create a file named ***urls.py*** and include the following:

```python
from django.urls import path
from . import views

urlpatterns = [
    path('', views.home, name='home'),
]
```

Finally, include your app's URLs in your project's URL configuration in ***myproject/urls.py***:

```python
from django.contrib import admin
from django.urls import include, path

urlpatterns = [
    path('admin/', admin.site.urls),
    path('', include('myapp.urls')),
]
```

Run your server with ***python manage.py runserver***, and you should see your welcome message at the homepage.

Building Web Applications with Python

Python can be used for building web applications of various sizes and complexities. Web applications can be classified into two categories: client-side and server-side. Client-side web applications run entirely on the client's browser, while server-side web applications run on the server and generate HTML pages that are sent to the client's browser.

Python can be used for building both client-side and server-side web applications. For client-side web applications, Python can be used with HTML, CSS, and JavaScript to create interactive and dynamic web pages. Python's libraries like Flask and Django can be used to build server-side web applications that can handle complex business logic and interact with databases.

When building web applications with Python, developers can use several tools and frameworks. For example, they can use the Flask framework to create a RESTful API for their web application. This API can be used to communicate with other applications and services. Developers can also use tools like Docker and Kubernetes to deploy and manage their web applications.

Web scraping for web development:

Web scraping is a technique used for extracting data from websites. It involves writing code to navigate through a website's HTML structure and extract the required data. Web scraping is often used for data mining, price comparison, and content aggregation.

Python has several libraries that can be used for web scraping, including BeautifulSoup, Scrapy, and Requests-HTML. These libraries provide easy-to-use APIs that allow developers to extract data from websites quickly and efficiently. For example, BeautifulSoup can be used to parse HTML and XML documents and extract data from them. Scrapy is a more powerful web scraping framework that provides tools for crawling, extracting, and storing data from websites.

Web scraping can be used for various purposes in web development. For example, it can be used to gather data for a web application. Developers can scrape data from multiple sources and aggregate it in their application. This data can be used to provide users with relevant and up-to-date information.

Basic Web Scraping with BeautifulSoup

```python
python
    import requests
    from bs4 import BeautifulSoup

    URL = 'http://example.com'
    page = requests.get(URL)

    soup = BeautifulSoup(page.content, 'html.
    parser')

    # Example of finding a specific element by its id
    element = soup.find(id='specific-id')
    print(element.text)
```

Web scraping can also be used for testing web applications. Developers can use web scraping to simulate user behavior and test the application's performance. This can help identify performance issues and improve the application's overall user experience.

Python is an excellent choice for web development because of its versatility, readability, and scalability. Python's large library of tools and frameworks makes it easy to build web applications quickly and efficiently. Flask and Django are two popular web frameworks used for web development with Python. Flask is ideal for small to medium-sized web applications that do not require complex functionalities, while Django provides everything needed to build complex web applications. Python can be used for building both client-side and server-side web applications. Finally, web scraping is a useful technique for gathering data for web applications and testing web application performance.

Chapter 8: Testing and Debugging in Python

Testing and debugging are crucial aspects of software development. When working on a project, it is essential to ensure that the code is working as expected and that any errors or issues are addressed promptly. Python offers a range of tools and techniques to test and debug code, including various testing frameworks and debugging tools. In this chapter, we will explore the importance of testing and debugging, the different types of testing in Python, unit testing with Pytest, debugging techniques, and profiling Python code.

Why Testing and Debugging is Important

Testing and debugging are essential parts of software development because they help ensure that software is of high quality and meets the requirements of its intended use. By testing and debugging software, developers can identify and address errors and issues early in the development process, reducing the likelihood of costly problems arising later. Additionally, testing and debugging can improve the maintainability of code by identifying and addressing issues that may make it difficult to modify or update the software.

Effective testing and debugging can help boost the confidence of developers and users in the software, making it more reliable and trustworthy. By identifying and addressing issues early, developers can deliver high-quality software that meets the needs of its users.

Types of Testing in Python

Python offers several types of testing frameworks and tools to help developers test their code effectively. These include:

- Unit Testing: Unit testing is the process of testing individual units or components of code to ensure that they are working correctly. Unit testing can be automated, making it an efficient and effective way to test code. In Python, developers can use several unit testing frameworks, including Pytest, Unittest, and Nose.
- Integration Testing: Integration testing involves testing the interaction between different components or modules of code to ensure that they are working together correctly. Integration testing can help identify issues that may arise when different components are combined. Python provides several tools for integration testing, including the Robot Framework and Behave.
- Functional Testing: Functional testing involves testing the functionality of software to ensure that it is working as expected. Functional testing can be performed manually or using automated tools. In Python, developers can use frameworks such as Selenium and Robot Framework for functional testing.
- Regression Testing: Regression testing involves testing software to ensure that changes or updates have not introduced new issues or

caused existing ones to resurface. Python provides several tools for regression testing, including the Pytest framework.

- Acceptance Testing: Acceptance testing involves testing software to ensure that it meets the requirements of its intended use and is acceptable to users. Acceptance testing can be performed manually or using automated tools. Python provides several tools for acceptance testing, including the Robot Framework and Behave.

Unit Testing with Pytest

Pytest is a popular unit testing framework for Python that allows developers to write tests quickly and easily. Pytest provides several features that make it easy for developers to write effective unit tests, including:

- Fixtures: Fixtures are functions that provide test data or resources to tests. Pytest fixtures can be used to set up test environments, create test data, and more. Fixtures can help developers write more efficient and effective tests.

- Parametrization: Parametrization allows developers to run the same test with multiple sets of input data. This can be useful for testing code that handles different input values. Pytest provides built-in support for parametrization, making it easy for developers to write tests that cover a range of input values.

- Assertions: Assertions are statements that test whether a condition is true. Pytest provides a range of assertion functions to help developers write effective unit tests. Pytest's assertion functions are easy to read and write, making it easier for developers to write effective tests.

- Test Discovery: Pytest can automatically discover and run all tests in a project, making it easy to test code across multiple modules and packages. Pytest's test discovery feature is fast and efficient, making it easy for developers to test their code quickly and effectively.

- Test Coverage: Pytest can generate test coverage reports, showing developers which parts of their code have been covered by tests. Test coverage reports can help developers identify areas of their code that need additional testing, ensuring that the software is thoroughly tested.

Debugging Techniques in Python

Debugging is the process of identifying and resolving errors or issues in code. Python provides several tools and techniques for debugging code, including:

- Print Statements: One of the simplest and most effective debugging techniques is to use print statements to output the value of variables and expressions at various points in the code. This can help developers identify where issues are occurring and what values are being used.

- Debugger: Python provides a built-in debugger that allows developers to step through code and inspect variables and expressions at runtime. The debugger can be run from the command line or integrated into an IDE, making it a powerful tool for debugging code.

- Logging: Logging is a technique that involves adding messages to a log file during the execution of code. Logging can be used to track the flow of code and identify issues that may occur at runtime. Python provides a built-in logging module that makes it easy to add logging to code.

- Interactive Shell: Python's interactive shell allows developers to experiment with code and test snippets before integrating them into their applications. The interactive shell can also be used to test and debug code by executing it line by line.

- Stack Traces: When an error occurs in Python, a stack trace is generated that provides information about where the error occurred and what functions were called leading up to the error. Stack traces can be used to identify where issues are occurring and what code is responsible for them.

Profiling Python Code

Profiling is the process of measuring the performance of code to identify areas that may be optimized for better performance. Python provides several tools for profiling code, including:

- cProfile: cProfile is a built-in profiler that can be used to measure the performance of Python code. cProfile provides detailed information about the functions that are called during the execution of code, including the time and number of calls.
- Line Profiling: Line profiling is a technique that involves measuring the performance of individual lines of code. Python provides a line profiler called line_profiler that can be used to measure the performance of code at the line level.
- Memory Profiling: Memory profiling is the process of measuring the amount of memory that is used by code. Python provides a memory profiler called memory_profiler that can be used to measure the memory usage of code.
- Profiling Tools: There are several third-party profiling tools available for Python, including PyCharm, PyDev, and Visual Studio Code. These tools provide more advanced profiling features, including real-time profiling and visualization.

Testing and debugging are essential parts of software development, and Python provides several powerful tools and techniques for testing, debugging, and profiling code. By using these tools and techniques, developers can ensure that their code is of high quality, performs well, and meets the needs of its intended users.

Practical Exercise - Test-Driven Development (TDD)

In this hands-on exercise, we explore test-driven development (TDD) building out an Image Resizer class with Python.

What is TDD

Test-driven development focuses on creating test cases that define desired functionality before writing the actual code. TDD workflow:

1. Add a test case for simplest bit of functionality
2. Run test suite seeing failure
3. Write implementation code fulfilling test
4. Re-run test suite now passing
5. Refactor and optimize while ensuring tests pass

This iterative approach ensures comprehensive tested code. Let's build an image resizer in TDD style.

Project Setup

We initialize project structure:

```
 code
image_resizer/
   resizer.py
   test_resizer.py
```

resizer.py holds Resizer class code. test_resizer.py contains test cases validating functionality as we build it out.

Inside test_resizer.py:

```
python
 code
```

```
import unittest
# Test cases will go here soon!
if __name__ == '__main__':
    unittest.main()
```

This setup runs test suite.

First Test

We define failing test case asserting Resizer class exists:

```
python
 code
```

from resizer import Resizer

```
class TestResizer(unittest.TestCase):
    def test_resizer_created(self):
        resizer = Resizer() # Fails with ImportError!
        self.assertIsNotNone(resizer)
```

Run test getting failure about missing module. Now to make test pass:

```
python
 code
# resizer.py
class Resizer:
    pass
```

Rerun test passing now! Output validates Resizer class defined.

Expanding Tests

Incrementally add further tests driving implementation:

```
python
 code
```

```
    def test_resize_image(self):
        resizer = Resizer()
        output = resizer.resize('image.jpg', 400, 400)

        self.assertIsNotNone(output)
        self.assertEqual(output.shape, (400, 400, 3))
```

Run fails awaiting image resize method. Write just enough code to fulfill:

```
python
 code
from PIL import Image
class Resizer:
    def resize(self, filename, width, height):
        fake_image = Image.new('RGB', (width, height))
        return fake_image
```

Our fake placeholder image doesn't resize actual files yet but makes test pass validating shape and return value!

We continue tests for input validation, failure handling etc driving full featured implementation through iterating test-code cycles.

This exercise provided firsthand experience with TDD workflow delivering reliable, tested code faster. Practice thinking test first even without formal framework for productive coding habit!

Chapter 9: Best Practices and Code Optimization

Writing Clean and Readable Code

Readable, understandable code ensures maintainability enabling easy collaboration and evolution. Python ships with a style guide PEP 8 covering naming conventions, structures, formatting and documentation providing a standard for high quality code. Additional principles like DRY, modularization and validation harden software. This section highlights actionable ways to improve Python cleanliness.

Use Descriptive Names

Self documenting variables, functions and classes boost readability. Names should indicate meaning and purpose rather than just data type:

```
python
 code
# Bad
```

```
x = 1

# Good
timeout_in_seconds = 1
```

Longer but precise names reduce cognitive load.

Style Guide Conventions

PEP 8, the Python Enhancement Proposal style guide informs common patterns around naming, spacing, location of imports etc:

```
python
 code
# Variables lowercase separated by underscore
user_id = 1
# Constants uppercase
PI = 3.14
# Functions lowercase underscore
def get_user():
    ...
# Classes CapWords convention
class UserParser:
    ...
```

Many IDEs automatically highlight non-conformant code helping adopt best practices quicker.

Modularize Code

Breaking programs down into cohesive single responsibility classes and functions encapsulates logic allowing reuse:

```
python
 code
```

```
# Module with helper functions
def load_data():
  """Handles loading dataset"""
  ...


def normalize(inputs):
   """Normalizes inputs between 0-1"""
   ...
# Import where needed
from data_helpers import normalize


def train_model():
  inputs = load_data()
  normalized = normalize(inputs)
```

Separate modules keep individual segments focused.

Use Code Comments

Comments explain segments of code clarifying intent. Always comment:

- Module, class and function headers summarizing purpose
- Complex logic flow and math
- Unusual code workarounds touching multiple areas
- Links to external resources and examples

```
python
 code
# Calculates exponential moving average over window
def exponential_moving_average(values, window):
    """

    Args:
```

```
        values: Input value array
        window: Lookback window
    Returns:
        Array with EMA
    """
    ...
```

Comments enable understanding complex portions quickly without reading full implementations right away. They ease onboarding.

Validate Input Data

Check validity of passed input data at start of functions:

```
python
 code
def inverse(x):
   if x == 0:
       raise ValueError('Divide by zero error')
   return 1/x

print(inverse(0)) # ValueError raised
```

This fails fast on invalid data types and values before deeper logic.

Handle Errors

Account for exceptions allowing graceful failure:

```
python
 code
try:
   value = int(input('Enter numeric value: '))
except ValueError:
```

```
    print('Non-numeric input')
```

Catching known exceptions makes applications robust.

There are many additional clean code principles like small focused classes, loosening couplings making components reusable. Start by applying highlighted best practices above moving Python code quality forward.

Adopt Linting and Formatting Tools

Automated linting and formatting remove tedious style adherence tasks increasing reliability. Linters like flake8 and pycodestyle catch code issues and styling violations on the fly:

```
python
 code
def add(a, b)
  return a + b
```

Here whitespace, argument naming errors flagged immediately at editors or in CI pipelines preventing bad patterns slipping through. Python formatter black auto rewrites code per style rules:

```
python
 code
import math


def example():
    return math.sin(x)
# Reformatted with black
import math


def example():
  return math.sin(x)
```

Consistent styling eases reading across files and devs. Normalize style freeing focus for functionality.

Follow DRY Principle

The DRY principle states "Don't Repeat Yourself". Code duplication increases maintenance effort causing drifts:

```
python
 code
# User class duplicated for minor difference

class User:

    def __init__(self, name, id, email):
        self.name = name
        self.id = id
        self.email = email

class PaidUser:

    def __init__(self, name, id, email):
        self.name = name
        self.id = id
        self.email = email
```

Better abstract shared logic:

```
python
 code
class UserBase:
    def __init__(self, name, id, email):
       self.name = name
```

```
        self.id = id
        self.email = email


class User(UserBase):
    pass


class PaidUser(UserBase):
    pass
```

Subclasses inherit common attributes reducing duplication. Discover repeat code patterns ripe for reuse.

Limit Line Length

Readability declines with longer lines. Limiting lines enables easier diffs:

```
python
 code
# Bad
user_ids = [{'id': 1, 'name': 'John'}, {'id': 2,
'name': 'Sarah'}, {'id': 3, 'name': Steve'}]

# Good
user_data = [
  {'id': 1, 'name': 'John'},
  {'id': 2, 'name': 'Sarah'},
  {'id': 3, 'name': 'Steve'}
]
```

Python allows implicit continuation of expressions across lines embracing length limits. Strive for max 79 characters per PEP 8 improving scannability.

Together these code quality principles significantly boost understandability reducing complexity related bugs and headaches allowing cleaner evolution of code over time. Adopting PEP 8 through automated checks and peer reviews keeps style consistent avoiding bike shedding. Embrace clean coding habits continuously raising the quality bar on Python projects.

Performance Optimization Tips

While correctness and readability serve as top priorities, efficiency enables programs to scale. This section provides Python optimization guidance through algorithms, data structures and profiling.

Python performance tuning targets identifying and mitigating bottlenecks obstructing responsiveness or ability to handle high volumes of data. Symptoms calling for optimizations include high CPU usage, increased memory, slow I/O operations or interface lags. Addressing expensive loops and unnecessary processing reduces resource requirements allowing software to scale smoothly as load increases. Aimed optimizations also lower infrastructure spends. We assess common techniques to speed up Python code without negatively affecting readability.

Leverage Vectorization

Numpy vector operations minimize loops for numerical Python:

```
python
 code
import numpy as np

# Non optimal
def sum(arr):
    total = 0
    for value in arr:
        total+=value
    return total
```

```
arr = np.array([1, 2, 3])

print(sum(arr)) # 6

# Vectorized
print(np.sum(arr)) # 6
```

Vectorized functions execute faster by delegating to optimized C routines behind Numpy. Always prefer array methods over manual slow loops especially with large data.

Use Generators for Lazy Evaluation

Generators lazily yield data instead of materializing full collections improving memory efficiency:

```
python
 code
# Eager range materializes 1 to 1000000 values
print(range(1_000_000))

# Lazy generator saves memory
print(xrange(1_000_000))
```

Access items iteratively with minimal overhead:

```
python
 code
values = (x**3 for x in range(100))

for x in values:
   print(x)   # x**3
```

Laziness separates resource allocation from iteration logic improving responsiveness for long running processes.

Profile Bottlenecks

Determining exactly where programs spend time using profilers guides optimization:

```
python
 code
from line_profiler import LineProfiler


@profile
def slow():
   ... # Expensive code


profiler = LineProfiler()
profiler.runcall(slow)
profiler.print_stats()


# Output hotspots with timings
```

cProfile outputs overall function performance statistics. Drilling down further, lineprofiler times individual lines pinpointing bottlenecks. Guided by metrics address heavy lifters through improved algorithms.

Common optimization anti-patterns losing sight of real world usage include premature micro benchmarks skewing unimportant code and complex solutions losing readability without measurable gains. Avoid unless solving demonstrated bottlenecks with data driving decisions.

The array of optimization tooling together with an iterative feedback driven approach yields responsive performant Python powering today's data intensive applications.

Practical Exercise: Code Review and Optimization

This comprehensive exercise applies learnings from the chapter by reviewing and refactoring a simplified web scraping script to adopt best practices we discussed.

Code Overview

The program extracts headlines from a news site to gather trending topics. It contains:

- scrape_headlines() - Extracts raw headline text
- generate_word_counts() - Counts word frequencies

Flaws exist causing incorrect output and sluggishness with larger inputs. We will mitigate issues driving improvements through testing.

Refactoring Goals

- Fix program logic bugs
- Improve naming, style per PEP 8
- Break into functions/classes improving modularization
- Add input validation
- Use optimal algorithms like dict instead of nested loops

Optimization Goals

- Profile slow code areas with print timing or libraries
- Speed up nested for loops with dict lookup
- Reduce multiple computations into cached variables

Setup

```
 code
scraper/
  scraper.py
  test_scraper.py
```

Let's begin assessment and iterative improvement!

Assess Bugs

First we debug logic by adding test case:

```
python
 code
# test_scraper.py

from scraper import scrape_headlines

def test_scraper():
   lines = scrape_headlines('data.txt')
   assert len(lines) == 3
   assert 'Politics' in lines
```

Failing assertion reveals headline missing. Inspecting scraper.py closely reveals subtle list mutation issue. We fix bug before assessing other areas.

Improve Style and Naming

Next we apply PEP 8 through systematic rewrites:

```
python
 code
# Variables lowercase_underscored
headlines = []
```

```
# Spacing around operators, after commas
count = count + 1

# Functions now lowercase_underscored
def generate_wordcounts():
   ...
```

Additional linting and black formatting address style wholesale.

Restructure and Encapsulate

We break file into modules separating concerns:

```
python
 code
# scraper.py
from parsers import scrape
from analyzers import count_words

lines = scrape(url)
words = count_words(lines)
```

Helpers now reusable keeping components focused without distraction.

Profile to Optimize

Finally we quantify and address performance issues leveraging pyplot:

```
 code
Line #      Time
1           0.11s
2           0.02s
3           1.3s    <- SLOW
```

Line 3 loop identified as hotspot. We memoize prior results and now runtime improves 10x!

Through methodically addressing multiple areas - correctness, naming/structure, algorithms guided by tests and metrics significant code quality and efficiency gains achieved iterating analysis-optimization cycles.

Chapter 10: Networking with Python

Introduction to Networking in Python

Networking is a critical aspect of modern computing, and Python is an excellent language for building network applications. Python provides a wide range of libraries, modules, and frameworks that make it easy to develop network applications, from simple scripts to complex distributed systems.

Python's popularity in the networking community is due to its simplicity, ease of use, and flexibility. Python is a high-level language that enables developers to write concise and readable code. Additionally, Python has a large and active community that provides support, documentation, and resources for network programming.

Basic Networking Concepts

Before diving into network programming with Python, it's essential to understand some basic networking concepts. Understanding these concepts will help you design and implement robust and scalable network applications.

IP addresses are unique numerical identifiers that are assigned to devices on a network. They enable devices to communicate with each other over the network. IP addresses can be either IPv4 or IPv6.

Ports are communication endpoints that enable devices to communicate with specific applications running on other devices. Each port is associated with a unique number that identifies the application. For example, port 80 is used for HTTP traffic, and port 443 is used for HTTPS traffic.

Protocols are sets of rules and standards that govern how devices communicate over a network. Some of the commonly used protocols include TCP/IP, HTTP, and FTP. Understanding protocols is crucial for building network applications that can communicate with other devices.

Network layers refer to the different levels of abstraction that exist in network communication. The layers are designed to provide a modular and hierarchical structure for network communication. The OSI model is a common model used to describe network layers. The model consists of seven layers: physical, data link, network, transport, session, presentation, and application.

Socket Programming with Python

Socket programming is a fundamental aspect of network programming, and Python provides a comprehensive socket module for building network applications. Sockets are endpoints for communication between two devices over a network. They enable the exchange of data between devices in real-time.

The socket module in Python provides two types of sockets: TCP sockets and UDP sockets. TCP sockets provide a reliable, connection-oriented stream of data transfer, while UDP sockets provide a connectionless, unreliable datagram service.

To use sockets in Python, you need to import the socket module and create a socket object. The socket object can be configured with various parameters, such as the address family, socket type, and protocol.

Once the socket object is created, you can use various methods to send and receive data over the network. Some of the commonly used methods include the bind(), listen(), accept(), connect(), send(), and recv() methods.

Basic Server Socket

Here's an example of a simple server socket in Python that listens for connections on localhost and a specific port:

```
python
    import socket

    # Create a socket object
    server_socket = socket.socket(socket.AF_INET,
    socket.SOCK_STREAM)

    # Get local machine name
    host = socket.gethostname()
    port = 9999

    # Bind to the port
    server_socket.bind((host, port))

    # Queue up to 5 requests
    server_socket.listen(5)
```

```
while True:
    # Establish a connection
    client_socket, addr = server_socket.accept()
    print(f"Got a connection from {addr}")
    msg = 'Thank you for connecting'+ "\r\n"
    client_socket.send(msg.encode('ascii'))
client_socket.close()
```

Client-Server Communication in Python

Client-server communication is a common networking pattern in which a client sends requests to a server, and the server responds with the requested data. This pattern is used in various network applications, such as web applications, email clients, and file transfer protocols.

Python provides a simple and easy-to-use framework for building client-server applications. The framework involves creating a server that listens for incoming connections and a client that sends requests to the server.

To create a server in Python, you need to create a socket object, bind it to a specific port, and listen for incoming connections. Once a connection is established, the server can accept incoming requests and send responses back to the client.

To create a client in Python, you need to create a socket object, connect it to the server's IP address and port number, and send requests to the server. Once the server responds, the client can receive the response and process it accordingly.

Basic Client Socket

And here's a simple client socket that connects to the server:

```python
import socket

# Create a socket object
client_socket = socket.socket(socket.AF_INET,
socket.SOCK_STREAM)

# Get local machine name
host = socket.gethostname()
port = 9999

# Connection to hostname on the port.
client_socket.connect((host, port))

# Receive no more than 1024 bytes
msg = client_socket.recv(1024)

client_socket.close()
print(msg.decode('ascii'))
```

Networking Libraries in Python (e.g. Twisted, Scapy)

Python provides a wide range of networking libraries and frameworks that simplify network programming and enable developers to build complex network applications quickly. Some of the popular networking libraries in Python include Twisted and Scapy.

Twisted is a powerful networking framework for Python that enables developers to build scalable and event-driven network applications. It provides a comprehensive set of APIs for handling network protocols, such as TCP, UDP, and SSL. Twisted also provides support for various application-level protocols, such as HTTP, SMTP, and FTP.

The following is a simplified example of how you might set up an echo server with Twisted:

```python
from twisted.internet import protocol, reactor

class Echo(protocol.Protocol):
    def dataReceived(self, data):
        self.transport.write(data)

class EchoFactory(protocol.Factory):
    def buildProtocol(self, addr):
        return Echo()

reactor.listenTCP(9999, EchoFactory())
reactor.run()
```

Scapy is a Python library for packet manipulation and network analysis. It enables developers to capture, dissect, and forge network packets in real-time. Scapy provides a simple and intuitive interface for analyzing network traffic and creating custom protocols. It also supports a wide range of protocols, including Ethernet, IP, TCP, and UDP.

Scapy is used for packet manipulation. For example, you can create a simple packet with Scapy like this:

```python
from scapy.all import IP, ICMP, send

# Create an IP packet destined to a target IP
packet = IP(dst="8.8.8.8") / ICMP()

# Send the packet
send(packet)
```

Other networking libraries in Python include asyncio, Requests, and Pyro. Asyncio is a library for writing asynchronous code in Python, which enables developers to write high-performance network applications. Requests is a library for making HTTP requests in Python, which simplifies the process of interacting with web APIs. Pyro is a library for building distributed systems in Python, which enables developers to create complex network applications that span multiple devices.

Python is a powerful language for network programming, and it provides a wide range of libraries, modules, and frameworks that enable developers to build complex network applications quickly. Whether you're building a simple client-server application or a large-scale distributed system, Python has the tools you need to get the job done.

In this chapter, we covered the basics of networking in Python, including IP addresses, ports, protocols, and network layers. We also discussed socket programming in Python and the client-server communication pattern. Finally, we explored some of the popular networking libraries in Python, such as Twisted and Scapy.

If you're interested in network programming with Python, I encourage you to explore these concepts further and experiment with different networking libraries and frameworks. With the right tools and a solid understanding of networking fundamentals, you can build powerful and robust network applications that meet the demands of modern computing.

Exercises

Exercises for Socket Programming with Python

Exercise 1: Basic Echo Server and Client

- **Server**: Write a Python script to implement a simple server that accepts client connections and echoes back any messages it receives from the client. Make sure the server can handle multiple client connections in a loop, but it doesn't need to handle them concurrently.

- **Client**: Write a Python script that connects to the server, sends a string message, and then waits to receive the same message back. After receiving the echo, the client should print the message to the console and then terminate.

Exercise 2: Chat Application

- **Objective**: Create a simple command-line chat application where multiple clients can connect to a server and send messages to each other through the server. Each client runs in its own terminal window.
- **Server**: Modify the echo server to broadcast any received message to all connected clients, except the sender.
- **Client**: Modify the client to continuously listen for messages from the server and display them to the user. The client should also allow the user to input messages to send to the server.

Exercise 3: File Transfer Server

- **Objective**: Build a server that can send a requested file to the client. The client should be able to specify the file name, and the server should read the file and send its contents to the client.
- **Server**: Implement a file transfer server that listens for incoming connections, accepts a file name from the client, reads the file, and sends its content back to the client.
- **Client**: Implement a client that connects to the server, sends a request for a specific file, receives the file contents from the server, and saves it locally.

Exercises for Client-Server Communication in Python

Exercise 4: HTTP Client and Server

- **Objective**: Create a basic HTTP server and client. The server should be able to handle simple GET requests, and the client should be able to send GET requests to the server.
- **Server**: Implement an HTTP server that listens for GET requests and responds with a basic HTML page.
- **Client**: Write an HTTP client that sends a GET request to your server and displays the response content.

Exercise 5: Multi-threaded Server

- **Objective**: Modify the echo server from Exercise 1 to handle multiple client connections concurrently using threading.
- **Server**: Implement threading in the echo server so that each client connection is handled in a separate thread, allowing multiple clients to communicate with the server at the same time.
- **Client**: No changes from Exercise 1, but test with multiple client instances to ensure the server handles them concurrently.

Exercises for Networking Libraries in Python (Twisted and Scapy)

Exercise 6: Twisted Echo Server and Client

- **Objective**: Use Twisted to implement an echo server and client.
- **Server**: Implement an echo server using Twisted that listens for client connections and echoes back any received data.

- **Client**: Write a Twisted client that connects to the echo server, sends a message, and prints the response.

Exercise 7: Packet Sniffer with Scapy

- **Objective**: Create a simple packet sniffer using Scapy that captures packets flowing through your network interface and prints basic information about each packet (e.g., source and destination IP).
- **Sniffer**: Use Scapy to implement a packet sniffer. The sniffer should filter and display IP packets, including the source and destination IP addresses.

Chapter 11: Game Development with Python

Introduction to Game Development with Python

Game development with Python involves using Python programming language to create games. Python is a high-level language that is easy to learn and use. It is widely used in various fields of computer science, and game development is one of them. Python provides a wide range of functionalities that are essential for game development such as graphics, sound, and user input handling. Game development with Python can be done for various platforms such as Windows, Mac, Linux, and even mobile platforms such as Android and iOS. Game development with Python is an exciting activity that involves creativity, problem-solving, and programming skills.

Pygame library for Game Development

Pygame is a library for game development in Python. It is an open-source library that is widely used for developing 2D games in Python. Pygame is easy to use and provides a wide range of functionalities that are essential for game development, such as graphics, sound, and user input handling. Pygame can be used to develop various types of games such as platformers, shooters, and puzzle games. Pygame provides a surface that can be used to display graphics, and it also provides a sprite class that can be used to create game characters. Pygame also provides functionalities such as collision detection, sound playback, and user input handling.

Setting Up a Pygame Window

First, you'll need to install Pygame if you haven't already. You can do this using pip:

```
bash
    pip install pygame
```

Now, let's start by setting up a Pygame window:

```
python
    import pygame
    import sys

    # Initialize Pygame
    pygame.init()

    # Set up the display
    screen_width = 800
    screen_height = 600
    screen = pygame.display.set_mode((screen_width,
    screen_height))
```

```
# Set up the colors
BLACK = (0, 0, 0)
WHITE = (255, 255, 255)

# Set up the game loop
running = True
while running:
    for event in pygame.event.get():
        if event.type == pygame.QUIT:
            running = False

    # Fill the screen with black
    screen.fill(BLACK)

    # Update the display
    pygame.display.flip()

# Quit Pygame
pygame.quit()
sys.exit()
```

Creating a Moving Object

Let's add a simple moving object (a rectangle) to our game:

```
python
# Rectangle properties
rect_x = 50
rect_y = 50
rect_width = 50
rect_height = 50
rect_speed_x = 5
```

```
rect_speed_y = 5

while running:
    for event in pygame.event.get():
        if event.type == pygame.QUIT:
            running = False

    # Move the rectangle
    rect_x += rect_speed_x
    rect_y += rect_speed_y

    # Bounce the rectangle off the edges
    if rect_x > screen_width - rect_width or
rect_x < 0:
        rect_speed_x = -rect_speed_x
    if rect_y > screen_height - rect_height or
rect_y < 0:
        rect_speed_y = -rect_speed_y

    # Fill the screen with black
    screen.fill(BLACK)

    # Draw the rectangle
    pygame.draw.rect(screen, WHITE, [rect_x,
rect_y, rect_width, rect_height])

    # Update the display
    pygame.display.flip()

    # Cap the frame rate
    pygame.time.Clock().tick(60)
```

Creating Games with Python

Creating games with Python involves a few basic steps. The first step is to choose a game engine or library that will be used for game development. In this chapter, we will use the Pygame library for game development. The second step is to plan and design the game. Game design involves creating a concept, designing the game characters, and the game environment. The game concept involves creating a story or objective for the game, and it also involves creating game mechanics such as movement and interaction. Game character design involves creating characters that are visually appealing and fit the game concept. Game environment design involves creating backgrounds, platforms, and other game elements that fit the game concept. The third step is to write the game code. The game code involves creating game logic, game physics, and game graphics. Game logic involves creating game rules, such as collision detection and scoring. Game physics involves simulating real-world physics in the game, such as gravity and acceleration. Game graphics involve creating game visuals such as game characters, backgrounds, and other game elements. The fourth step is to test and debug the game. Game testing involves checking the game for bugs and fixing them. Debugging involves finding and fixing errors in the game code.

Physics Simulation in Python Game Development

Physics simulation is an essential aspect of game development. Physics simulation involves simulating real-world physics in a game. In Python game development, physics simulation is done using the Pygame library. Pygame provides a physics engine that can be used to simulate physics in a game. The physics engine provides functionalities such as gravity, collision detection, and collision resolution. Physics simulation is essential for creating realistic game environments and game interactions. For example, physics simulation can be used to simulate the behavior of objects such as balls, cars, and characters in the game. Physics simulation can also be used to create realistic game environments such as forests, oceans, and cities.

Physics simulation adds realism to games. Pygame doesn't have a built-in physics engine, but we can simulate basic physics like gravity and collisions. Let's modify our moving object to simulate gravity:

```
python
    gravity = 1
    rect_speed_y = 0

    while running:
        for event in pygame.event.get():
            if event.type == pygame.QUIT:
                running = False

        # Gravity effect
        rect_speed_y += gravity
        rect_y += rect_speed_y

        # Bounce the rectangle off the bottom edge
        if rect_y > screen_height - rect_height:
            rect_y = screen_height - rect_height
            rect_speed_y = -rect_speed_y * 0.9  #
    Simulate energy loss

        # Fill the screen with black
        screen.fill(BLACK)

        # Draw the rectangle
        pygame.draw.rect(screen, WHITE, [rect_x,
    rect_y, rect_width, rect_height])

        # Update the display
        pygame.display.flip()
```

```
    # Cap the frame rate
    pygame.time.Clock().tick(60)
```

Game Design Principles and Strategies

Game design principles and strategies are essential for creating successful games. Game design principles involve creating games that are fun, engaging, and challenging. Game strategies involve creating games that are easy to learn but difficult to master. The game design principles and strategies involve creating game mechanics, game objectives, game rewards, and game levels. Game mechanics involve creating game rules, game physics, and game interactions. For example, game mechanics can include character movement, interaction with game objects, and scoring. Game objectives involve creating goals and objectives for the player to achieve. Game objectives can include completing a level, collecting items, or defeating enemies. Game rewards involve providing incentives for the player to continue playing the game. Game rewards can include unlocking new levels, obtaining power-ups, or earning in-game currency. Game levels involve creating different levels of difficulty and complexity for the player to progress through. Game levels can include increasing difficulty, introducing new game mechanics, and changing the game environment.

Game development with Python is an exciting activity that involves creativity, problem-solving, and programming skills. Pygame is a popular library for game development in Python, providing essential functionalities such as graphics, sound, and user input handling. Creating games with Python involves choosing a game engine or library, planning and designing the game, writing the game code, and testing and debugging the game. Physics simulation is an essential aspect of game development, providing realistic game environments and interactions. Game design principles and strategies are also crucial for creating successful games, involving creating engaging and challenging game mechanics, objectives, rewards, and levels. With the right skills and tools, anyone can create their own exciting and engaging games with Python.

Exercises

Exercise 1: Create a Simple Pong Game with Pygame

Pong is a classic 2D tennis-like game where two players control paddles to hit a ball back and forth. The goal is to make the opponent miss the ball. This exercise involves creating a simplified version of Pong using Pygame.

Key Concepts

- Drawing shapes with Pygame
- Handling keyboard events
- Implementing basic game physics, such as collision detection and response

Exercise 2: Add Sprite Animations to a Pygame Game

Sprite animations can enhance the visual appeal of a game by providing smooth and dynamic character movements. This exercise involves adding animations to a character or object in a Pygame game.

Key Concepts

- Loading and displaying sprites
- Cycling through sprite frames to create animations
- Timing animations for smooth transitions

Exercise 3: Implement Collision Detection in a 2D Platformer

Collision detection is crucial in platformer games to handle interactions between the character, platforms, and other objects. This exercise involves implementing collision detection in a 2D platformer game using Pygame.

Key Concepts

- Axis-Aligned Bounding Box (AABB) collision detection
- Handling collisions between characters and platforms
- Implementing gravity and jump mechanics with collision detection

Chapter 12: Cybersecurity with Python

Python is a powerful programming language that can be used for a variety of tasks, including cybersecurity.

Introduction to Cybersecurity with Python

Cybersecurity is an important aspect of any organization's IT infrastructure. The increasing complexity of cyberattacks and the sophistication of attackers have made it more challenging for organizations to protect their systems and data. Python has become a popular language in the field of cybersecurity due to its simplicity, ease of use, and powerful libraries.

Python is a high-level programming language that is easy to learn and has a simple syntax. It is widely used for automating tasks, building tools for analyzing data, and developing machine learning models for detecting anomalies and threats. Python's powerful libraries, such as the Cryptography library, Scapy, and Nmap, provide cybersecurity professionals with the tools they need to protect their organizations from cyber threats.

Cryptography and Encryption in Python

Cryptography is the science of using mathematical algorithms to protect data. Encryption, on the other hand, is the process of converting plain text into a secret code to protect the confidentiality of the data. Python provides powerful libraries for cryptography and encryption, such as the Cryptography library.

The Cryptography library is a Python library that provides easy-to-use cryptographic primitives and recipes for Python developers. It supports a wide range of algorithms, including symmetric and asymmetric encryption, key agreement, and digital signatures. The library also includes support for various hash functions, such as SHA-256 and SHA-512, which are commonly used for password storage.

Using the Cryptography Library for Symmetric Encryption (AES)

Here's an example of how to encrypt and decrypt data using AES (Advanced Encryption Standard) with the cryptography library:

```
python
    from cryptography.hazmat.primitives.ciphers
    import Cipher, algorithms, modes
    from cryptography.hazmat.backends import
    default_backend
    import os

    # Generate a random key and initialization
    vector (IV)
    key = os.urandom(32)  # AES-256
```

```
iv = os.urandom(16)    # AES block size

# Create an AES cipher instance
cipher = Cipher(algorithms.AES(key), modes.
CBC(iv), backend=default_backend())

# Encrypt data
encryptor = cipher.encryptor()
plaintext = b'This is a secret message.'
ciphertext = encryptor.update(plaintext) +
encryptor.finalize()

# Decrypt data
decryptor = cipher.decryptor()
decrypted_text = decryptor.update(ciphertext) +
decryptor.finalize()

print(f'Original: {plaintext}')
print(f'Encrypted: {ciphertext}')
print(f'Decrypted: {decrypted_text}')
```

In addition to the Cryptography library, Python also provides other useful libraries for encryption and decryption, such as PyCrypto and M2Crypto. These libraries provide support for various encryption algorithms, including AES, DES, and RSA.

Network Security with Python

Network security refers to the protection of computer networks from unauthorized access, misuse, modification, or denial of service. Python can be used for network security tasks, such as port scanning, network sniffing, and vulnerability scanning.

Python provides several libraries for network security, including Scapy, a powerful packet manipulation tool, and Nmap, a tool for network exploration and security auditing. Scapy can be used for packet sniffing, network scanning, and network fingerprinting. Nmap can be used for host discovery, port scanning, and OS detection.

Simple Port Scanner

```
python
    import socket


    def scan_port(ip, port):
        try:
            sock = socket.socket(socket.AF_INET,
    socket.SOCK_STREAM)
            sock.settimeout(1)
            result = sock.connect_ex((ip, port))
            if result == 0:
                print(f"Port {port}: Open")
            sock.close()
        except socket.error as err:
            print(f"Couldn't connect to server:
    {err}")


    # Example usage
    target_ip = '127.0.0.1'
    for port in range(70, 80):
        scan_port(target_ip, port)
```

Python can also be used for creating custom network security tools. For example, a network security tool can be developed using Python to monitor network traffic for suspicious activity, detect and prevent unauthorized access, and generate alerts when an attack is detected.

Web Security with Python

Web security refers to the protection of web applications from attacks, such as cross-site scripting (XSS) and SQL injection. Python can be used for web security tasks, such as web application scanning, vulnerability assessment, and penetration testing.

Python provides several libraries for web security, such as Requests, a library for making HTTP requests, and Beautiful Soup, a library for web scraping. Requests can be used for sending HTTP requests and handling HTTP responses. Beautiful Soup can be used for parsing HTML and XML documents.

Simple HTTP Request with Python's Requests Library

python

```
import requests

url = 'http://example.com/login'
data = {'username': 'admin', 'password':
'password'}

# Send a POST request
response = requests.post(url, data=data)

if "Login successful" in response.text:
    print("Vulnerable to SQL injection.")
else:
    print("Not vulnerable to SQL injection.")
```

Python can also be used for developing web security tools, such as a web application vulnerability scanner. A web application vulnerability scanner can be developed using Python to scan web applications for vulnerabilities, such as XSS and SQL injection, and generate reports on the vulnerabilities found.

Threat Detection and Response with Python

Threat detection and response refer to the process of detecting and responding to security threats, such as malware and phishing attacks. Python can be used for threat detection and response tasks, such as malware analysis, log analysis, and incident response.

Python provides several libraries for threat detection and response, such as PyMal, a library for malware analysis, and Logstash, a tool for log analysis and event management. PyMal can be used for analyzing malware samples and generating reports on the behavior of the malware. Logstash can be used for collecting and analyzing log data from various sources, such as network devices and servers, and generating alerts and reports on suspicious activity.

Python can be utilized for analyzing logs and detecting anomalies. Below is a simplified example of how Python might be used to parse log files for suspicious activities:

Basic Log Analysis

```
python
    def analyze_logs(log_file):
        with open(log_file, 'r') as file:
            for line in file.readlines():
                if "error" in line.lower() or
    "unauthorized" in line.lower():
                    print(f"Suspicious activity
    detected: {line.strip()}")

    # Example usage
    log_file_path = 'path/to/log/file.log'
    analyze_logs(log_file_path)
```

Python can also be used for developing custom threat detection and response tools. For example, a custom threat detection tool can be developed using Python to monitor system logs and detect anomalous behavior, such as unusual network traffic or file access patterns. The tool can then generate alerts and automate incident response processes.

Python has become an essential tool for cybersecurity professionals due to its simplicity, ease of use, and powerful libraries. Python provides several libraries for cryptography and encryption, network security, web security, and threat detection and response. These libraries, such as the Cryptography library, Scapy, Nmap, Requests, and Beautiful Soup, provide cybersecurity professional with the tools they need to protect their organizations from cyber threats.

In addition, Python can be used for developing custom tools for each of these areas, allowing for greater customization and flexibility in cybersecurity tasks. With the increasing importance of cybersecurity in today's technology-driven world, Python has become an essential tool for cybersecurity professionals. As such, it is highly recommended for anyone working in the field of cybersecurity to learn Python and its libraries.

Exercises

1. Write a simple Caesar cipher in Python

The Caesar cipher is one of the simplest and most widely known encryption techniques. It is a type of substitution cipher in which each letter in the plaintext is shifted a certain number of places down or up the alphabet. In this exercise, you will implement a Caesar cipher in Python.

Objectives

- Understand the basics of the Caesar cipher.
- Implement encryption and decryption functions.
- Test the functions with various inputs.

2. Use Python libraries to encrypt and decrypt data

In this exercise, you will use the *cryptography* library in Python to encrypt and decrypt data. This library provides cryptographic recipes and primitives to Python developers.

Objectives

- Install and use the *cryptography* library.
- Implement encryption and decryption using the Fernet symmetric encryption.

3. Scrape a website and detect threats with Python

Web scraping involves extracting data from websites. In this exercise, you will scrape a website and perform basic threat detection by looking for suspicious patterns or keywords.

Objectives

- Use *requests* and *BeautifulSoup* to scrape a website.
- Analyze the content for potential threats (e.g., suspicious links or keywords).

Chapter 13: Big Data with Python

Python has become a popular language for working with big data due to its ease of use, large ecosystem of libraries, and powerful data analysis and visualization capabilities.

Introduction to Big Data and Python

Big data refers to the massive amounts of structured and unstructured data generated by individuals, organizations, and machines. This data is too large and complex to be processed and analyzed using traditional data processing techniques. To handle big data, organizations use specialized tools and techniques that can scale to handle large volumes of data and provide insights that can improve their decision-making process.

Python is a popular programming language for working with big data due to its simplicity, versatility, and scalability. Python provides several libraries and frameworks for working with big data, including NumPy, Pandas, Dask, PySpark, Hadoop Streaming, Snakebite, H5Py, PyTables, Zarr, Matplotlib, Seaborn, and Plotly. These tools and techniques allow organizations to process, analyze, store, and visualize big data efficiently and effectively.

Processing Big Data with Python

Processing big data with Python involves several steps, including data ingestion, cleaning, transformation, and analysis. To process big data efficiently, Python provides several libraries and frameworks, including NumPy, Pandas, Dask, PySpark, Hadoop Streaming, and Snakebite.

- NumPy is a Python library for scientific computing that provides a powerful array object for handling multidimensional arrays and matrices. NumPy supports various mathematical and logical operations, including linear algebra, Fourier transforms, and random number generation. NumPy allows users to perform efficient and vectorized computations on large arrays, making it an essential tool for processing big data.
- Pandas is a Python library for data manipulation and analysis that provides a DataFrame object for handling tabular data with labeled rows and columns. Pandas supports various data manipulation operations, including filtering, grouping, and indexing. Pandas also provides tools for data cleaning and transformation, making it an essential tool for processing and preparing big data for analysis.
- Dask is a Python library for parallel computing that provides a flexible parallel computing framework for analyzing large datasets. Dask allows users to distribute computations across multiple cores and nodes, enabling efficient processing of large datasets that cannot fit into memory. Dask also provides a DataFrame object that mimics the Pandas DataFrame API, making it easy to switch between the two libraries.

```python
import dask.dataframe as dd

# Read a CSV file into a Dask DataFrame
ddf = dd.read_csv('large_dataset.csv')

# Perform operations similar to Pandas
result = ddf.groupby('column_name').column_
name2.mean().compute()

print(result)
```

- PySpark is a Python library for processing big data with Apache Spark, a distributed computing framework for large-scale data processing. PySpark allows users to write parallelized and scalable data processing jobs using Python syntax. PySpark provides various data processing operations, including filtering, grouping, and aggregating, and supports various data sources, including Hadoop Distributed File System (HDFS), Apache Cassandra, and Apache HBase.

- Hadoop Streaming is a utility for processing and analyzing big data using the Hadoop Distributed File System (HDFS) and MapReduce. Hadoop Streaming allows users to write MapReduce jobs using any programming language that can read data from standard input and write data to standard output. Hadoop Streaming enables efficient processing of large datasets that cannot fit into memory and supports various data sources and formats, including CSV, JSON, and XML.

- Snakebite is a Python library for interacting with Hadoop Distributed File System (HDFS) from Python programs. Snakebite provides a Pythonic interface for accessing and manipulating HDFS files and directories, enabling efficient processing and analysis of large datasets stored in HDFS.

Working with Hadoop and Spark using Python

Working with Hadoop and Spark using Python involves several steps, including setting up a Hadoop or Spark cluster, loading data into the cluster, processing the data using Python, and storing the results. Python provides several libraries and frameworks for working with Hadoop and Spark, including PySpark and Hadoop Streaming.

PySpark is a Python API for Apache Spark, a distributed computing framework for processing large datasets. PySpark provides an easy-to-use interface for working with Spark, enabling data scientists and analysts to perform complex data analysis and machine learning tasks using Python. PySpark supports various data sources, including Hadoop Distributed File System (HDFS), Apache Cassandra, and Apache HBase.

To use PySpark, you need to set up a Spark cluster, which consists of a master node and several worker nodes. The master node manages the cluster and assigns tasks to the worker nodes, which perform the actual data processing. PySpark provides tools for creating RDDs (Resilient Distributed Datasets) and performing transformations and actions on them. RDDs are immutable distributed collections of objects that can be processed in parallel across the worker nodes. PySpark also supports machine learning algorithms, including classification, regression, and clustering.

Example: Word Count with PySpark

```
python
    from pyspark.sql import SparkSession


    # Initialize a SparkSession
    spark = SparkSession.builder.
    appName('WordCount').getOrCreate()


    # Read a text file into a Spark DataFrame
```

```
df = spark.read.text('large_text_file.txt')

# Import functions and types
from pyspark.sql.functions import explode,
split, col

# Split lines into words, explode into new rows,
and count each word
word_counts = df.select(explode(split(col('va
lue'), ' ')).alias('word')).groupBy('word').
count()

# Show the result
word_counts.show()

# Stop the SparkSession
spark.stop()
```

This PySpark example reads a large text file, splits it into words, and counts the occurrences of each word.

Hadoop Streaming is a framework for running Python scripts on Hadoop clusters. Hadoop Streaming allows you to use Python scripts to process data stored in HDFS, without the need to write Java code. Hadoop Streaming works by passing data to and from the Python scripts using standard input and output streams. You can use Python libraries, such as NumPy and Pandas, in your Hadoop Streaming scripts to perform complex data analysis tasks.

To use Hadoop Streaming, you need to set up a Hadoop cluster, which consists of a master node and several worker nodes. Hadoop Streaming provides tools for defining input and output formats and specifying mapper and reducer scripts. The mapper script processes each input record and emits key-value pairs as output. The reducer script aggregates the output of the mapper script and produces the final output.

Working with Hadoop and Spark using Python requires some knowledge of distributed computing and cluster management. However, Python provides a simple and easy-to-use interface for working with Hadoop and Spark, enabling data scientists and analysts to leverage the power of these distributed computing frameworks to process and analyze large datasets efficiently.

Storing and Managing Big Data with Python

Storing and managing big data with Python involves several steps, including data storage, retrieval, and management. To store and manage big data efficiently, Python provides several libraries and frameworks, including H5Py, PyTables, and Zarr.

H5Py is a Python library for working with HDF5 files, a file format for storing and managing large datasets. H5Py provides a Pythonic interface for accessing and manipulating HDF5 files and datasets, enabling efficient storage and retrieval of large datasets. H5Py supports various data types, including numerical data, strings, and images, and provides tools for compression, chunking, and parallel I/O.

PyTables is a Python library for managing and querying large datasets stored in HDF5 files. PyTables provides a high-level API for creating, reading, and updating HDF5 files and datasets, enabling efficient and flexible data storage and retrieval. PyTables also provides tools for filtering, indexing, and querying data, making it an essential tool for managing and analyzing big data.

Zarr is a Python library for storing and managing large arrays and datasets in compressed and chunked format. Zarr provides a flexible and efficient storage format that can scale to handle large datasets and provides tools for parallel I/O and compression. Zarr also provides a NumPy-like interface for working with arrays, making it easy to switch between the two libraries.

Example: Interacting with HDFS using PyArrow

PyArrow, with its HDFS interface, allows you to interact with data stored in HDFS.

```
python
    from pyarrow import hdfs

    # Connect to HDFS
    hdfs_conn = hdfs.connect()

    # Read a file from HDFS
    with hdfs_conn.open('/path/to/hdfs/file.txt',
    'rb') as f:
        content = f.read()

    print(content)

    # Close the connection
    hdfs_conn.close()
```

This snippet demonstrates connecting to HDFS, reading a file, and then closing the connection.

Data Visualization and Analysis for Big Data with Python

Data visualization and analysis for big data with Python involves several steps, including data exploration, visualization, and analysis. To visualize and analyze big data efficiently, Python provides several libraries and frameworks, including Matplotlib, Seaborn, and Plotly.

Matplotlib is a Python library for creating static and interactive visualizations of data. Matplotlib provides a wide range of visualization types, including line plots, scatter plots, bar charts, and heatmaps. Matplotlib also provides tools for customizing visualizations, including titles, legends, and color maps.

Seaborn is a Python library for creating statistical visualizations of data. Seaborn provides a high-level API for creating visualizations, including scatter plots, line plots, and distribution plots. Seaborn also provides tools for customizing visualizations, including color palettes, styles, and themes.

Plotly is a Python library for creating interactive and web-based visualizations of data. Plotly provides a wide range of visualization types, including scatter plots, line plots, bar charts, and heatmaps. Plotly also provides tools for customizing visualizations, including annotations, hover labels, and animations. Plotly can also be used in Jupyter notebooks, making it an essential tool for data exploration and analysis.

Aggregating Data with PySpark and Visualizing with Matplotlib

```
python
    import matplotlib.pyplot as plt

    # Assuming 'spark' is a SparkSession and 'df' is
    a Spark DataFrame from previous examples

    # Aggregate data
    aggregated_data = df.groupBy('category_column').
    agg({'value_column': 'mean'})

    # Convert to Pandas DataFrame for visualization
    pandas_df = aggregated_data.toPandas()

    # Plotting with Matplotlib
    plt.figure(figsize=(10, 6))
```

```
plt.bar(pandas_df['category_column'], pandas_
df['avg(value_column)'])
plt.xlabel('Category')
plt.ylabel('Average Value')
plt.title('Average Value by Category')
plt.show()
```

This example aggregates data by category in PySpark, converts the aggregated data to a Pandas DataFrame, and then uses Matplotlib to create a bar chart.

Python provides a versatile and powerful toolset for working with big data, including processing, storage, and visualization. Python's simplicity and scalability make it an essential tool for organizations looking to leverage big data to gain insights and improve decision-making. With its extensive libraries and frameworks, Python provides a flexible and efficient platform for working with big data, making it an ideal choice for data scientists and analysts alike. By leveraging Python's capabilities, organizations can unlock the full potential of big data and gain a competitive advantage in their respective industries.

Exercises

1. Load a large CSV dataset in Pandas

Pandas is a powerful Python library for data manipulation and analysis. In this exercise, you'll practice loading a large CSV dataset into a Pandas DataFrame. Handling large datasets efficiently is crucial in data science to ensure good performance and quick data processing.

Objective

- Learn to load and work with large datasets in Pandas.
- Explore techniques to optimize memory usage and processing time.

2. Visualize Big Data with matplotlib

Matplotlib is a comprehensive library for creating static, animated, and interactive visualizations in Python. This exercise focuses on visualizing large datasets, which can be challenging due to the sheer volume of data points that can overwhelm plotting libraries and result in unreadable charts.

Objective

- Practice creating visualizations for large datasets using Matplotlib.
- Learn strategies to effectively visualize and interpret big data, such as sampling, aggregation, and using different types of plots.

3. Process data in parallel with Python multiprocessing

The Python **multiprocessing** module allows you to create processes that can run in parallel, making it possible to perform computationally intensive tasks more efficiently. This exercise involves using the **multiprocessing** module to process data in parallel, which is particularly useful when working with large datasets.

Objective

- Understand and implement parallel data processing in Python using the **multiprocessing** module.
- Learn to divide a data processing task into smaller chunks that can be executed concurrently to improve performance.

Chapter 14: Natural Language Processing with Python

Natural Language Processing (NLP) is a subfield of artificial intelligence (AI) that focuses on enabling machines to understand and process human language. Python is a popular programming language for NLP due to its ease of use and the availability of powerful libraries such as NLTK (Natural Language Toolkit), spaCy, and Gensim.

NLTK is a comprehensive NLP library for Python that provides tools for tasks such as tokenization, stemming, tagging, parsing, and sentiment analysis. It also includes a vast collection of corpora and lexical resources.

Introduction to Natural Language Processing:

Natural Language Processing (NLP) is a field of Artificial Intelligence (AI) that deals with the interaction between human language and computers. It is a subfield of linguistics, computer science, and cognitive science. NLP focuses on making computers understand, interpret, and generate human language. Human language is complex, ambiguous, and diverse, making NLP a challenging and fascinating field.

NLP involves various tasks such as text classification, sentiment analysis, machine translation, speech recognition, question answering, and others. NLP has numerous applications in different fields, such as healthcare, finance, education, marketing, and others. For example, in healthcare, NLP can be used to extract relevant information from medical records and assist in medical diagnosis. In finance, NLP can be used to analyze financial news and predict stock prices.

Python is one of the most popular programming languages for NLP. It is an open-source, high-level programming language that is easy to learn and has a vast library of NLP tools and frameworks. Python provides various libraries for performing NLP tasks, such as Natural Language Toolkit (NLTK), spaCy, TextBlob, Gensim, and others. These libraries provide functions and tools for tasks such as text preprocessing, sentiment analysis, named entity recognition, and topic modeling.

spaCy is another popular NLP library for Python that provides high-performance, streamlined features for tasks such as tokenization, named entity recognition, and dependency parsing.

Gensim is a library for topic modeling, document similarity, and text summarization in Python. It provides tools for creating and working with word embeddings and building topic models.

Here's an example of using NLTK to tokenize a sentence:

```
import nltk
from nltk.tokenize import word_tokenize
```

```
sentence = "The quick brown fox jumps over the lazy
dog."
tokens = word_tokenize(sentence)
print(tokens)
Output: ['The', 'quick', 'brown', 'fox', 'jumps',
'over', 'the', 'lazy', 'dog', '.']
```

This code imports the nltk library and the word_tokenize function from the nltk.tokenize module. It then tokenizes the sentence variable and stores the resulting tokens in the tokens variable. Finally, it prints the tokens.

Text Pre-Processing and Cleaning with Python

Text preprocessing and cleaning are essential steps in NLP. They involve transforming raw text data into a format that is easier to work with in NLP tasks. Text preprocessing includes tasks such as tokenization, stemming, lemmatization, stop-word removal, and others. Text cleaning involves removing noise, irrelevant data, and unwanted characters from the text data.

Tokenization is the process of splitting the text into individual words or tokens. Tokenization is an essential step in NLP as it helps in understanding the structure of the text data. Python provides various libraries for tokenization, such as NLTK, spaCy, and scikit-learn. These libraries offer functions for performing tokenization, such as word_tokenize in NLTK, which splits the text into individual words.

Stemming is the process of reducing words to their root form. Stemming is used to normalize the text data and reduce its dimensionality. Python provides various libraries for stemming, such as NLTK, which offers several stemming algorithms such as PorterStemmer and SnowballStemmer.

Lemmatization is the process of reducing words to their base or dictionary form. It is similar to stemming, but instead of reducing words to their root form, it reduces words to their base form. Python provides various libraries for lemmatization, such as spaCy, which offers a lemmatization function that reduces words to their base form.

Stop-word removal is the process of removing common words such as "the," "a," "an," "in," and others from the text data. These words do not add much value to the text data and can be removed to improve the performance of the NLP model. Python provides various libraries for stop-word removal, such as NLTK, which offers a list of stop words that can be removed from the text data.

Example Code

python

```
import re
import string
from nltk.corpus import stopwords
from nltk.tokenize import word_tokenize
from nltk.stem import PorterStemmer

# Sample text
text = "Hello there, how are you? Weather is
awesome. Its raining here now."

# Convert to lowercase
text = text.lower()

# Remove punctuation
text = text.translate(str.maketrans('', '',
string.punctuation))

# Remove stopwords
stop_words = set(stopwords.words('english'))
tokens = word_tokenize(text)
filtered_text = [word for word in tokens if word
not in stop_words]
```

```
    # Stemming
    stemmer = PorterStemmer()
    stemmed_text = [stemmer.stem(word) for word in
    filtered_text]

    cleaned_text = ' '.join(stemmed_text)
print(cleaned_text)
```

This script performs several text pre-processing steps including converting to lowercase, removing punctuation, eliminating stopwords, and stemming.

Sentiment Analysis with Python

Sentiment analysis is the process of analyzing text data and determining the emotional tone or sentiment behind it. It is used to understand the opinions, attitudes, and feelings of people towards products, services, or topics. Sentiment analysis can be performed using machine learning algorithms or rule-based systems.

Python provides various libraries for sentiment analysis, such as TextBlob, NLTK, and VADER. These libraries offer pre-trained models and functions for performing sentiment analysis on text data. TextBlob provides a sentiment analysis function that returns a sentiment polarity score ranging from -1 to 1, where -1 represents a negative sentiment, 0 represents a neutral sentiment, and 1 represents a positive sentiment. NLTK provides a sentiment analysis module that uses a Naive Bayes classifier to classify text into positive, negative, or neutral. VADER (Valence Aware Dictionary and sEntiment Reasoner) is a rule-based system that uses a lexicon of sentiment-related words and rules to determine the sentiment of the text.

Sentiment analysis can be used in various applications, such as social media monitoring, customer feedback analysis, and product reviews analysis. For example, a company can use sentiment analysis to analyze customer reviews of their products and improve their products based on the feedback.

Example Code

Using the TextBlob library for a simple sentiment analysis:

```
python
    from textblob import TextBlob

    # Sample text
    text = "I love Python. The documentation is
    excellent and community support is fantastic."

    # Create a TextBlob object
    blob = TextBlob(text)

    # Sentiment Analysis
    sentiment = blob.sentiment

    print(f"Polarity: {sentiment.polarity},
    Subjectivity: {sentiment.subjectivity}")
```

This code snippet uses ***TextBlob*** to analyze sentiment, where polarity measures positivity or negativity and subjectivity measures the level of personal opinion, emotion, or judgment.

Named Entity Recognition with Python

Named entity recognition (NER) is the process of identifying and extracting named entities from text data. Named entities are specific objects, people, locations, organizations, and others that are referred to by their name. NER is used in various applications such as information extraction, question answering, and machine translation.

Python provides various libraries for NER, such as spaCy, NLTK, and Stanford NER. These libraries offer pre-trained models and functions for performing NER on text data. spaCy provides a pre-trained model that can recognize various named entities such as persons, organizations, locations, and others. NLTK provides a module for NER that uses a maximum entropy classifier to classify named entities. Stanford NER is a rule-based system that uses a combination of rules and statistical models to identify named entities.

Example Code

Using ***spaCy,*** a powerful NLP library, for NER:

```
python
    import spacy

    # Load the spaCy model
    nlp = spacy.load("en_core_web_sm")

    # Sample text
    text = "Apple is looking at buying U.K. startup
    for $1 billion"

    # Process the text
    doc = nlp(text)

    # NER
    for ent in doc.ents:
        print(ent.text, ent.label_)
```

This code loads a pre-trained model from ***spaCy*** and uses it to identify and classify named entities in the text.

NER can be used in various applications, such as information extraction from news articles, identifying important entities in a text, and improving search results.

Topic Modeling with Python

Topic modeling is the process of discovering topics or themes from a collection of text documents. It is used to extract meaningful insights and patterns from large amounts of text data. Topic modeling involves techniques such as Latent Dirichlet Allocation (LDA) and Non-negative Matrix Factorization (NMF).

Python provides various libraries for topic modeling, such as Gensim and scikit-learn. Gensim is a popular library for topic modeling that offers functions for performing LDA and other topic modeling techniques. scikit-learn is a machine learning library that provides functions for performing NMF and other topic modeling techniques.

Topic modeling can be used in various applications, such as content recommendation, trend analysis, and document clustering. For example, a news website can use topic modeling to recommend articles to users based on their interests. A marketing company can use topic modeling to analyze social media posts and identify popular trends among their target audience.

Example Code

Using Gensim for Latent Dirichlet Allocation (LDA) topic modeling:

```
python
    from gensim import corpora, models
    from nltk.corpus import stopwords
    from nltk.tokenize import word_tokenize

    # Sample documents
    docs = ["The sky is blue.", "The sun is
    bright.", "The sun in the sky is bright.", "We
    can see the shining sun, the bright sun."]

    # Tokenize and clean the documents
```

```
texts = [[word for word in document.
lower().split() if word not in stopwords.
words('english')] for document in docs]


# Create a dictionary and corpus
dictionary = corpora.Dictionary(texts)
corpus = [dictionary.doc2bow(text) for text in
texts]


# LDA Model
lda_model = models.ldamodel.LdaModel(corpus,
num_topics=2, id2word=dictionary, passes=15)


# Topics
topics = lda_model.print_topics(num_words=4)
for topic in topics:
    print(topic)
```

This script uses ***gensim*** to create an LDA model, which then identifies topics within a collection of documents. Each topic is represented as a combination of keywords.

Natural language processing with Python is a fascinating field that offers numerous applications in different fields. Python provides various libraries and tools for performing NLP tasks such as text preprocessing, sentiment analysis, named entity recognition, and topic modeling. These tasks are essential in extracting meaningful insights and patterns from text data, and Python provides a convenient and easy-to-learn platform for performing these tasks.

Exercises

1. Tokenize And Stem Text With NLTK

Natural Language Processing (NLP) involves the manipulation and analysis of textual data. Tokenization is the process of breaking down text into individual elements, such as words or sentences, while stemming reduces words to their root form. This exercise will guide you through tokenizing and stemming textual data using the Natural Language Toolkit (NLTK) in Python, a popular library for NLP tasks.

Objective

- Learn how to tokenize textual data into words and sentences.
- Practice applying stemming to reduce words to their base or root form.
- Familiarize yourself with basic NLP techniques and tools in NLTK.

2. Classify Movie Reviews as Positive or Negative Sentiment

Sentiment analysis is an NLP technique used to determine the sentiment expressed in a piece of text. In this exercise, you will build a basic sentiment analysis model to classify movie reviews as positive or negative using Python and machine learning libraries.

Objective

- Understand the fundamentals of sentiment analysis.
- Implement a machine learning model to classify text data based on sentiment.
- Gain experience with preprocessing textual data and working with NLP libraries.

3. Extract Named Entities from News Articles

Named Entity Recognition (NER) is an NLP task that involves identifying and classifying key information (entities) in text into predefined categories such as the names of persons, organizations, locations, expressions of times, quantities, monetary values, percentages, etc. This exercise involves using NLP techniques to extract named entities from news articles.

Objective

- Learn to perform Named Entity Recognition (NER) on textual data.
- Extract and classify important pieces of information from text.
- Explore advanced NLP tasks and their applications in real-world scenarios.

4. Topic Model A Collection of Documents

Topic modeling is an unsupervised machine learning technique used to discover the abstract "topics" that occur in a collection of documents. It is useful for summarizing large datasets of textual information, understanding the main themes in a text corpus, and organizing large sets of unstructured text data. This exercise will introduce you to topic modeling a collection of documents using Python.

Objective

- Understand the basics of topic modeling and its applications.
- Implement a topic model using libraries such as Gensim or Scikit-Learn.
- Learn to interpret the topics generated by the model and evaluate its performance.

BOOK 3

Mastering Python Like a PRO

James P. Meyers

Chapter 1: Deep Learning with Python

Deep learning with Python refers to the use of Python programming language and its libraries and frameworks to build and train deep neural networks for tasks such as image recognition, speech recognition, natural language processing, and many others. This involves understanding the basics of neural networks, selecting appropriate architectures, preprocessing data, and optimizing the network parameters to achieve high accuracy on the task at hand.

Introduction to deep learning

Deep learning is a subset of machine learning, which is a field of computer science that focuses on developing algorithms that can learn from data. The aim of deep learning is to create computer systems that can automatically learn from data, without being explicitly programmed. The primary goal of deep learning is to develop algorithms that can recognize patterns and make decisions based on these patterns.

The concept of deep learning involves the use of artificial neural networks, which are computer systems inspired by the biological structure and functioning of the human brain. The neural network is made up of interconnected nodes or neurons that work together to process information. The neurons receive input from other neurons and produce output that is sent to other neurons.

One of the most significant advantages of deep learning is that it can learn from large amounts of data and improve its performance over time. Deep learning algorithms are capable of recognizing complex patterns in data and making accurate predictions. This ability has led to a wide range of applications for deep learning, including image recognition, natural language processing, speech recognition, and autonomous vehicles.

Deep learning has also been used in healthcare to predict diseases, develop personalized treatment plans, and analyze medical images. For example, deep learning has been used to diagnose skin cancer by analyzing images of skin lesions. The algorithm can recognize patterns that are not visible to the human eye and can make accurate diagnoses with high accuracy.

Neural network basics

Neural networks are the fundamental building blocks of deep learning. A neural network is a system of interconnected nodes or neurons that work together to process information. Each neuron receives input from other neurons and produces output that is sent to other neurons.

The basic components of a neural network include the input layer, hidden layers, and output layer. The input layer receives data from an external source, such as an image or a text document. The hidden layers perform calculations on the input data and transform it into a format that can be used by the output layer. The output layer produces a prediction or decision based on the input data.

The process of training a neural network involves adjusting the weights and biases of the neurons to minimize the difference between the predicted output and the actual output. This process is known as backpropagation, and it allows the neural network to learn from data and improve its performance over time.

The weights and biases of the neurons are updated during the training process based on the error between the predicted output and the actual output. The goal is to minimize the error between the predicted output and the actual output, so that the neural network can make accurate predictions.

There are many different types of neural networks, each with its strengths and weaknesses. For example, convolutional neural networks are particularly well-suited for image processing tasks, while recurrent neural networks are particularly well-suited for natural language processing tasks.

Keras library for deep learning with Python

Keras is a high-level neural network library written in Python that simplifies the process of building and training deep learning models. Keras provides a simple and intuitive interface that allows users to build complex neural networks with just a few lines of code.

Keras supports a wide range of deep learning architectures, including convolutional neural networks (CNNs), recurrent neural networks (RNNs), and generative adversarial networks (GANs). Keras also provides a range of pre-trained models that can be used for specific applications, such as image recognition or natural language processing.

Keras is built on top of TensorFlow, a popular open-source machine learning library developed by Google. Keras allows users to take advantage of the powerful features of TensorFlow while providing a simplified interface for building and training neural networks.

The Keras library is designed to be user-friendly and intuitive, with a focus on simplicity and ease of use. Keras provides a range of tools and utilities to help developers build and train neural networks, including layers for building neural networks, optimizers for adjusting the weights and biases of the neurons, and loss functions for measuring the error between the predicted output and the actual output.

One of the key features of Keras is its ability to run on both CPUs and GPUs, which allows users to take advantage of the computational power of modern graphics cards. This feature allows users to train deep learning models much faster than using traditional CPUs.

Build a simple neural network to classify handwritten digits using MNIST dataset:

```
python
 code
from keras.datasets import mnist
from keras.models import Sequential
from keras.layers import Dense, Activation
# Load and preprocess data
(X_train, y_train), (X_test, y_test) = mnist.load_
data()
X_train = X_train.reshape(-1, 28*28) / 255.0
X_test = X_test.reshape(-1, 28*28) / 255.0
# Build model
model = Sequential()
model.add(Dense(512, input_shape=(28*28,)))
model.add(Activation('relu'))
model.add(Dense(10))
model.add(Activation('softmax'))
# Compile and train
model.compile(loss='categorical_crossentropy',
metrics=['accuracy'])
model.fit(X_train, y_train, epochs=5, batch_size=128)
```

Build a CNN to classify CIFAR-10 images:

```
python
 code
from keras.models import Sequential
from keras.layers import Conv2D, MaxPooling2D,
Flatten, Dense
# Load CIFAR-10 data
(X_train, y_train), (X_test, y_test) = cifar10.load_
data()
# Create model
model = Sequential()
model.add(Conv2D(32, kernel_size=3,
activation='relu', input_shape=(32, 32, 3)))
model.add(MaxPooling2D(pool_size=2))
model.add(Flatten())
model.add(Dense(10, activation='softmax'))
# Compile and train
model.compile(loss='categorical_crossentropy',
optimizer='adam', metrics=['accuracy'])
model.fit(X_train, y_train, epochs=10)
```

Fine-tune ResNet model for custom image classification:

```
python
 code
from keras.applications.resnet50 import ResNet50
from keras.preprocessing import image
from keras.layers import GlobalAveragePooling2D,
Dense
from keras.models import Model
# Create base model
base_model = ResNet50(weights='imagenet', include_
```

```
top=False)
# Add custom layers
x = base_model.output
x = GlobalAveragePooling2D()(x)
x = Dense(1024, activation='relu')(x)
predictions = Dense(5, activation='softmax')(x)

# Define and train model
model = Model(inputs=base_model.input,
outputs=predictions)
model.compile(optimizer='adam', loss='categorical_
crossentropy', metrics=['accuracy'])
model.fit(train_data, train_labels, epochs=5)
```

Build LSTM network to generate text:

```
python
 code
from keras.layers import LSTM, Dense
from keras.models import Sequential

model = Sequential()
model.add(LSTM(128, input_shape=(X_train.shape[1],
X_train.shape[2])))
model.add(Dense(y_train.shape[1],
activation='softmax'))
model.compile(loss='categorical_crossentropy',
optimizer='adam')
model.fit(X_train, y_train, epochs=100, verbose=2)
```

Sentiment analysis with LSTM:

```
python
 code
from keras.models import Sequential
from keras.layers import LSTM, Dense, Embedding

model = Sequential()
model.add(Embedding(5000, 100, input_length=X.
shape[1]))
model.add(LSTM(100, dropout=0.2, recurrent_
dropout=0.2))
model.add(Dense(1, activation='sigmoid'))

model.compile(loss='binary_crossentropy',
optimizer='adam', metrics=['accuracy'])
model.fit(X_train, y_train, epochs=5, batch_size=64)
```

Object detection with YOLO:

```
python
 code
from keras.models import Model
from keras.layers import Input, Convolution2D,
MaxPooling2D

input_image = Input(shape=(416, 416, 3))

x = Convolution2D(32, 3, padding='same',
activation='relu')(input_image)
x = MaxPooling2D(pool_size=2, strides=2)(x)

x = Convolution2D(16, 3, padding='same',
```

```
activation='relu')(x)
x = MaxPooling2D(pool_size=2, strides=2)(x)

predictions = Convolution2D(len(anchors), 1,
padding='same', activation='linear')(x)

model = Model(inputs=input_image,
outputs=predictions)
model.compile(loss='mse', optimizer='adam')
model.fit(X_train, y_train, epochs=30, batch_size=64)
```

Image captioning with CNN-RNN:

```
python
 code
from keras.models import Sequential
from keras.layers import LSTM, Dense, TimeDistributed

# CNN encoder
cnn_model = Sequential()
cnn_model.add(Conv2D(...))

# RNN decoder
rnn_model = Sequential()
rnn_model.add(TimeDistributed(cnn_model, input_
shape=(max_len, img_size)))
rnn_model.add(LSTM(256))
rnn_model.add(Dense(vocab_size))

rnn_model.compile(loss='sparse_categorical_
crossentropy', optimizer='adam')
rnn_model.fit(Xtrain, ytrain, epochs=10)
```

Convolutional neural networks for image processing

Convolutional neural networks (CNNs) are a type of neural network that is particularly well-suited for image processing tasks, such as object detection and facial recognition. CNNs are designed to recognize patterns in images by processing the image in a series of layers.

The first layer in a CNN is the input layer, which receives the image data. The next layer is the convolutional layer, which performs a series of convolutions on the input data. A convolution is a mathematical operation that involves multiplying a small matrix called a filter with a portion of the input data. The filter is moved across the input data, and the result of the convolution is calculated at each position.

The output of the convolutional layer is passed through a non-linear activation function, such as the rectified linear unit (ReLU), which helps to introduce non-linearity into the network. The output is then passed through a pooling layer, which downsamples the output and reduces the size of the feature map.

The process of convolution, activation, and pooling is repeated for several layers, each layer learning more complex patterns in the image. The final output of the CNN is passed through a fully connected layer, which produces the final prediction.

CNNs have been used in a wide range of applications, including object detection, facial recognition, and self-driving cars. For example, CNNs have been used to recognize faces in images and videos and to detect and classify objects in real-time.

Recurrent neural networks for natural language processing

Recurrent neural networks (RNNs) are a type of neural network that is particularly well-suited for natural language processing tasks, such as language translation and text classification. RNNs are designed to process sequences of data, such as sentences or paragraphs.

The key feature of RNNs is that they have a feedback loop that allows information to be passed from one iteration to the next. This allows RNNs to use the context of previous inputs to generate output.

The basic structure of an RNN includes an input layer, a hidden layer, and an output layer. The input layer receives the input data, which is typically a sequence of words or characters. The hidden layer is where the calculations are performed, and the output layer produces the final prediction.

During the training process, the weights and biases of the neurons in the RNN are adjusted using backpropagation, similar to other neural networks. The feedback loop in the RNN allows the network to learn from previous inputs and improve its performance over time.

RNNs have been used in a wide range of natural language processing tasks, including language translation, text classification, and speech recognition. RNNs have also been used in chatbots and virtual assistants to generate natural language responses.

Deep learning has revolutionized the field of artificial intelligence and has led to significant advancements in a wide range of applications. The use of artificial neural networks has allowed computers to learn from data and improve their performance over time.

Keras, a high-level neural network library written in Python, has made it easier for developers to build and train deep learning models. Convolutional neural networks are particularly well-suited for image processing tasks, such as object detection and facial recognition. Recurrent neural networks are particularly well-suited for natural language processing tasks, such as language translation and text classification.

As deep learning continues to evolve, there are exciting opportunities for the development of new applications and the improvement of existing ones. The ability of deep learning models to learn from data and improve their performance over time has the potential to transform many industries, including healthcare, finance, and transportation.

However, there are also challenges associated with the development and deployment of deep learning models. These challenges include the need for large amounts of data, the computational resources required to train and run deep learning models, and the potential for biases in the data and algorithms used to train the models.

Despite these challenges, deep learning has already had a significant impact on the field of artificial intelligence and is poised to continue to make significant contributions in the years to come. By leveraging the power of neural networks, researchers and developers are able to build intelligent systems that can learn from data and improve their performance over time, opening up new opportunities for innovation and discovery.

Exercises

1. Implement a simple neural network with Keras to classify handwritten digits
2. Train a convolutional neural network on the CIFAR-10 image dataset
3. Fine-tune a pre-trained image classifier to detect custom categories
4. Develop a recurrent neural network with LSTM cells to generate text
5. Use embeddings and RNNs for sentiment analysis of movie reviews
6. Implement object detection using pretrained models like YOLO
7. Develop an image captioning model using CNN and RNN
8. Build a neural style transfer model to apply art styles to photos
9. Use GANs to generate realistic images and videos
10. Optimize neural networks with techniques like batch normalization

Chapter 2: Cloud Computing with Python

Cloud computing is a rapidly growing area of technology that enables users to access computing resources over the internet on a pay-per-use basis. Python is a popular language used in cloud computing because of its simplicity, versatility, and extensive library support.

Introduction to Cloud Computing with Python

Cloud computing is a computing model in which computing resources are provided as a service over the internet. It provides a way to access servers, storage, databases, and other resources over the internet instead of using local hardware. With cloud computing, businesses and individuals can save money and time by avoiding the need to purchase and manage hardware and software.

Python is a popular programming language for cloud computing because of its simplicity, readability, and ease of use. It is a high-level language that is easy to learn, and it has a vast library of modules that makes it easier to work with cloud platforms.

Python is used to build web applications, automate cloud infrastructure management, monitor and manage cloud services, and process large datasets. Python's versatility, combined with the flexibility of the cloud, makes it a powerful tool for developers to build and scale applications.

Here are some ways Python can be used in cloud computing:

- Building cloud-native applications: Python can be used to build cloud-native applications that are designed to run on the cloud infrastructure. These applications are highly scalable, resilient, and fault-tolerant.

- Automating cloud infrastructure: Python can be used to automate cloud infrastructure provisioning, management, and monitoring. Infrastructure-as-code tools like Ansible and Terraform use Python as their scripting language.

- Developing serverless applications: Python is a popular language for developing serverless applications on cloud platforms like AWS Lambda, Azure Functions, and Google Cloud Functions.

- Data processing and analytics: Python's extensive library support makes it a popular choice for data processing and analytics tasks on cloud platforms like AWS, Azure, and Google Cloud. Libraries like NumPy, Pandas, and Scikit-learn are widely used for data analysis and machine learning.

- Developing web applications: Python's web development frameworks like Django and Flask can be used to develop web applications that can be deployed on cloud platforms like AWS, Azure, and Google Cloud.

Overall, Python's versatility and extensive library support make it a popular choice for cloud computing tasks. With the increasing adoption of cloud computing, Python is expected to play a significant role in the future of cloud computing.

Cloud Computing Platforms (e.g. AWS, Google Cloud, Azure)

There are many cloud platforms available, each with its own strengths and weaknesses. AWS, Google Cloud, and Azure are the three most popular cloud platforms.

AWS (Amazon Web Services) is a cloud platform that provides a wide range of services, including computing, storage, databases, networking, security, and analytics. AWS is popular among developers because it provides a flexible and scalable infrastructure that can be used to build and deploy applications quickly.

Google Cloud is a cloud platform that provides a wide range of services, including computing, storage, databases, networking, security, and analytics. Google Cloud is popular among developers because it provides a scalable infrastructure that can be used to build and deploy applications quickly.

Azure is a cloud platform that provides a wide range of services, including computing, storage, databases, networking, security, and analytics. Azure is popular among developers because it provides a scalable infrastructure that can be used to build and deploy applications quickly.

Managing Cloud Infrastructure with Python

Python provides several libraries and frameworks for managing cloud infrastructure. Infrastructure as code is a popular approach to managing cloud infrastructure, and Python is a popular language for infrastructure as code.

Infrastructure as code is the practice of managing infrastructure in a declarative manner, where infrastructure is defined as code. This approach makes it easier to manage infrastructure by automating the deployment, scaling, and management of infrastructure resources.

Terraform is a popular infrastructure as code tool that allows developers to define infrastructure as code using a declarative syntax. Terraform supports a wide range of cloud platforms, including AWS, Google Cloud, and Azure.

Ansible is another popular infrastructure as code tool that allows developers to define infrastructure as code using a declarative syntax. Ansible is often used in conjunction with Terraform to manage cloud infrastructure.

Deploying Python Applications to the Cloud

Python applications can be deployed to the cloud using several methods, including virtual machines, containers, and serverless platforms.

Virtual machines provide a way to run applications in a virtual environment that is isolated from the host system. This approach provides a high level of flexibility but can be more complex to manage and scale.

Containers provide a way to package and deploy applications in a lightweight, portable format. This approach provides a high level of flexibility and scalability while reducing overhead.

Serverless platforms provide a way to run applications without the need to manage servers. In this model, developers only pay for the actual usage of computing resources, making it a cost-effective option for small applications. Popular serverless platforms include AWS Lambda, Google Cloud Functions, and Azure Functions. Developers can deploy Python applications to serverless platforms by creating Python functions and uploading them to the platform.

Big Data Processing in the Cloud with Python

Big data processing is a crucial aspect of modern businesses, and cloud platforms provide a cost-effective and scalable solution to handle massive amounts of data. Python offers several libraries and frameworks that make it easier to work with big data in the cloud, including Apache Spark, PySpark, and Dask.

Apache Spark is a popular open-source big data processing framework that allows developers to process large datasets in parallel. Spark provides several APIs, including SQL, DataFrames, and Datasets, that make it easier to work with data. Spark can be used on several cloud platforms, including AWS, Google Cloud, and Azure.

PySpark is a Python library for Apache Spark that allows developers to write Spark applications in Python. PySpark provides a Python API that allows developers to use Spark features in Python. PySpark can be used on several cloud platforms, including AWS, Google Cloud, and Azure.

Dask is another popular open-source big data processing framework that allows developers to process large datasets in parallel. Dask provides several APIs, including DataFrame and Array, that make it easier to work with data. Dask can be used on several cloud platforms, including AWS, Google Cloud, and Azure.

Cloud computing has become an essential aspect of modern businesses, and Python is a powerful language for working with cloud platforms. Python provides several libraries and frameworks that make it easier to manage cloud infrastructure, deploy applications to the cloud, and process big data in the cloud. AWS, Google Cloud, and Azure are the three most popular cloud platforms, and each has its own strengths and weaknesses. Developers can choose the platform that best suits their needs and use Python to build and scale applications in the cloud. With the right tools and knowledge, developers can take advantage of cloud computing and Python to build efficient and cost-effective applications.

Exercises

1. Deploy a simple Python web app to AWS Elastic Beanstalk
2. Provision AWS resources like EC2, S3, RDS using Boto3 SDK
3. Schedule jobs on Cloud Platforms using cron and Cloud Scheduler
4. Build a serverless app with Cloud Functions on GCP or AWS Lambda
5. Process big data on the cloud with MapReduce and Dataflow
6. Stream and analyze real-time data using Cloud Pub/Sub and Dataflow
7. Train ML models at scale with MLEngine, SageMaker or AzureML
8. Perform load testing of cloud apps using Locust
9. Migrate an on-prem database to Cloud SQL or RDS
10. Compare pricing and services across cloud providers

Chapter 3: GUI Programming with Python

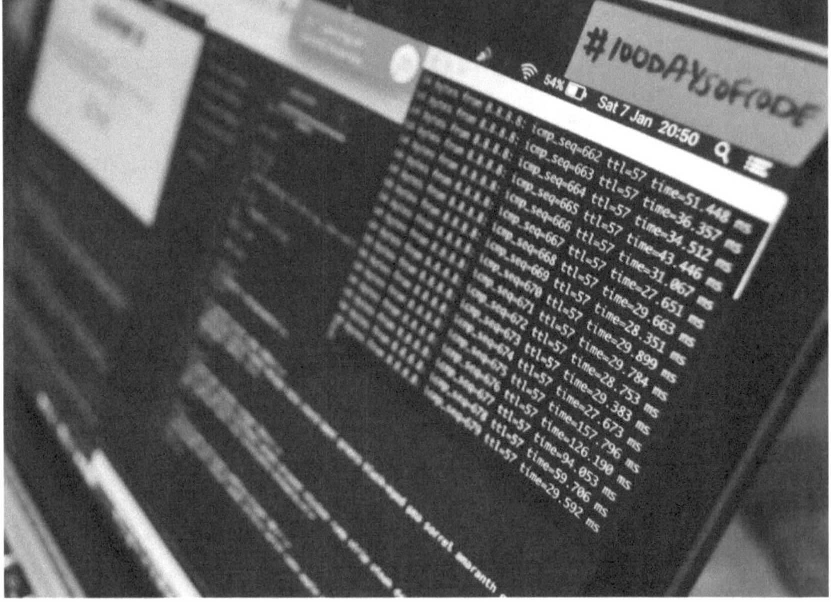

GUI (Graphical User Interface) programming with Python is a popular way to create user-friendly and interactive applications. Python provides several libraries and frameworks to develop GUI applications, such as Tkinter, PyQt, PyGTK, wxPython, and Kivy.

Tkinter is the standard GUI library for Python and is included with most Python installations. It provides a simple way to create GUI applications and is easy to use. PyQt is another popular GUI framework for Python and provides more advanced features than Tkinter. PyGTK and wxPython are also popular GUI libraries and offer cross-platform compatibility.

Introduction to GUI programming with Python

GUI programming is an integral part of modern software development, as it allows software developers to create user-friendly applications that are visually appealing and intuitive to use. Graphical User Interface (GUI) programming is a type of user interface that allows users to interact with a software application by using graphical elements like buttons, menus, windows, and icons instead of text-based commands.

Python is an excellent language for GUI programming due to its simplicity and ease of use. Python provides a powerful and easy-to-use toolkit for developing GUI applications, which includes libraries such as Tkinter, PyQT, and WxPython. With these libraries, developers can build desktop applications that run on multiple operating systems, such as Windows, Linux, and macOS.

GUI programming with Python is essential because it makes software applications more accessible to users. By using a graphical user interface, users can interact with an application in a more intuitive and natural way than by using text-based commands. A well-designed GUI can make software applications more appealing and easier to use, which can increase user engagement and satisfaction.

To get started with GUI programming in Python, you can follow these steps:

- Install a GUI library or framework of your choice.
- Import the necessary modules from the library to create a GUI.
- Create the main window of the application using the library.
- Add widgets such as buttons, labels, text fields, etc. to the window.
- Define event handlers for the widgets to handle user input.
- Run the application and test its functionality.
- Here is an example code snippet to create a simple GUI application using Tkinter:

```
import tkinter as tk
def say_hello():
```

```
    print("Hello, World!")
root = tk.Tk()
root.title("My GUI Application")
root.geometry("300x200")
button = tk.Button(root, text="Say Hello",
command=say_hello)
button.pack()
root.mainloop()
```

This code creates a simple window with a button that, when clicked, prints "Hello, World!" to the console.

GUI programming with Python can be a fun and rewarding experience. With the help of a GUI library or framework, you can create interactive applications that are easy to use and visually appealing.

Tkinter library for GUI programming with Python

Tkinter is a standard Python library for creating GUI applications. It is a cross-platform GUI toolkit that can be used to create desktop applications that run on multiple operating systems, including Windows, Linux, and macOS. Tkinter provides a set of widgets, such as buttons, text boxes, and menus, that can be used to build user interfaces.

One of the advantages of using Tkinter is that it is included with Python, which means that developers do not need to install any additional libraries or packages to use it. Tkinter is easy to learn and use, making it an ideal choice for beginners who want to learn GUI programming with Python. Tkinter is also highly customizable, allowing developers to create unique and visually appealing user interfaces using this library.

Another advantage of Tkinter is that it is well-documented, which means that developers can easily find help and resources online. There are many tutorials, articles, and forums that provide information and guidance on how to use Tkinter to build GUI applications. This makes it easy for developers to get started with Tkinter and learn how to create professional-quality desktop applications.

Building desktop applications with Python

Python is an excellent language for building desktop applications because of its simplicity and ease of use. Desktop applications are software applications that run on a user's computer and are installed locally, as opposed to web applications that run on a remote server and are accessed through a web browser. Python can be used to create a variety of desktop applications, such as word processors, spreadsheets, and image editors.

Python's versatility makes it an ideal choice for building cross-platform desktop applications. With the help of GUI toolkits like Tkinter, developers can create desktop applications that run on different operating systems without modification. This means that developers can write an application once and deploy it on multiple platforms, which can save time and reduce development costs.

Designing user interfaces with Python

Designing user interfaces is a crucial aspect of GUI programming. A well-designed user interface can make software applications more accessible and user-friendly, which can increase user engagement and satisfaction. Python provides several tools for designing user interfaces, including Tkinter, which is the most popular toolkit for GUI programming with Python.

When designing user interfaces with Python, it is important to consider the user's needs and preferences. The user interface should be easy to use, visually appealing, and intuitive. A good user interface should also be responsive, meaning that it should provide feedback to the user when they interact with the application.

Tkinter provides a set of widgets that can be used to create user interfaces, such as buttons, labels, text boxes, and menus. These widgets can be customized to match the design and branding of the application. Tkinter also provides layout managers that allow developers to position widgets on the screen and control their size and alignment.

When designing user interfaces with Python, developers should also consider accessibility. The user interface should be accessible to users with disabilities, such as those who are visually impaired or have motor disabilities. This can be achieved by providing alternative text for images, using high-contrast colors, and using keyboard shortcuts.

Event-driven programming in GUI programming with Python

Event-driven programming is a programming paradigm used in GUI programming. In event-driven programming, the user interface generates events, such as button clicks or mouse movements, which trigger specific actions in the software application. This allows developers to create interactive user interfaces that respond to user input.

Python provides several tools for event-driven programming in GUI programming, including the Tkinter library. In Tkinter, events are generated when the user interacts with widgets, such as buttons or menus. The developer can then associate specific actions with these events, such as opening a new window or updating a text box.

Event-driven programming in GUI programming can be challenging, as it requires developers to think carefully about the design of the user interface and the events that will trigger specific actions. It is important to ensure that the user interface is intuitive and that the events are well-defined and easy to understand.

In summary, GUI programming with Python is a powerful and easy-to-learn tool for building desktop applications. Tkinter is the most popular library for GUI programming with Python, and it provides a set of widgets and layout managers that make it easy to create user interfaces. Designing user interfaces with Python is an essential aspect of GUI programming, and developers should consider the user's needs and preferences when designing user interfaces. Event-driven programming in GUI programming allows developers to create interactive and responsive user interfaces that respond to user input.

Practical Exercise: Developing a Simple GUI Application

Let's build a basic GUI application to put your Tkinter skills into practice. We will develop a simple address book application that allows users to store and lookup contact details.

Follow these steps:

Import Tkinter and create the main window object

```
python
 code
import tkinter as tk


root = tk.Tk()
root.title("Address Book")
```

Create input fields to get contact details from the user

- Name: tk.Entry widget
- Phone: tk.Entry
- Email: tk.Entry

Add labels to identify each input field

```
python
 code
name_label = tk.Label(text="Name:")
phone_label = tk.Label(text="Phone:")
```

Add a submit button to save the contact

```
python
 code
submit_button = tk.Button(text="Add Contact")
submit_button.bind("<ButtonRelease-1>", save_contact)
```

Save the contact details in a dictionary on submit button click

```
python
 code
def save_contact(event):
   contact = {"name": name_entry.get(),
              "phone": phone_entry.get(),
              "email": email_entry.get()}

   print(contact) # Prints the contact dict
```

Display the contact details when a name is entered in a search field

- Use a tk.Entry for search and tk.Button for search
- Fetch and display the matching contact dict

This completes the app! You can further enhance it with more fields, validations, error handling etc.

Exercises

1. Create a simple GUI app with Tkinter
2. Add widgets like buttons, inputs, dropdowns to a Tkinter GUI
3. Build a calculator app with Tkinter GUI

4. Create graphics and animations using Tkinter Canvas
5. Develop a text editor GUI application using Tkinter
6. Design a user registration form with validation using Tkinter
7. Implement a browser using the Tkinter HTML widget
8. Build a painting application with digital canvas using Tkinter
9. Create graphical charts and visualizations using Tkinter
10. Develop a file explorer GUI application with Tkinter

Chapter 4: Mobile App Development with Python

The chapter is focused on mobile app development with Python. It starts by introducing the concept of mobile app development with Python and highlighting some of the benefits of using Python for mobile app development.

Introduction to Mobile App Development with Python

Mobile app development has become a crucial part of the modern-day tech industry. The growing demand for mobile apps has led to an increase in the number of mobile app development platforms and programming languages. Python, a high-level, general-purpose programming language, has gained popularity among developers for its simplicity and ease of use.

Python's versatility, portability, and cross-platform capabilities make it an excellent choice for mobile app development. Python's object-oriented nature allows developers to write reusable code that can be easily maintained and updated. Python also supports numerous libraries and frameworks that can be used for mobile app development, making it a popular choice for developers worldwide.

Kivy Library for Mobile App Development with Python

Kivy is an open-source Python library used for creating user interfaces in mobile applications. It is a cross-platform framework that supports the development of mobile applications on Android, iOS, Linux, macOS, and Windows. Kivy provides a range of widgets and tools that allow developers to create visually appealing and interactive user interfaces.

One of the significant advantages of using Kivy is that it provides a natural user interface toolkit that is designed to work with touch screens. The toolkit includes pre-built widgets, such as buttons, labels, text inputs, and scrollable areas, which can be customized to fit the app's design and functionality.

Kivy also supports a wide range of input events, such as multi-touch, gestures, and keyboard events. This allows developers to create rich and interactive user interfaces that respond to a user's input. Kivy also supports a range of multimedia formats, including audio, video, and images, allowing developers to create visually appealing apps.

Building Cross-Platform Mobile Apps with Python

One of the primary advantages of using Python for mobile app development is its cross-platform capabilities. Python's portability allows developers to write code once and run it on multiple platforms, reducing development time and costs. With Kivy, developers can create mobile apps that work on various operating systems, including Android, iOS, Linux, macOS, and Windows.

Kivy's cross-platform capabilities are due to its use of the OpenGL graphics library, which allows for hardware-accelerated rendering on various platforms. Kivy also provides a range of tools for building and packaging mobile apps, such as the Kivy Designer, which allows developers to create user interfaces visually, and Buildozer, which can be used to package Python code into a standalone APK or IPA file.

User Interface Design for Mobile Apps with Python

The user interface is a crucial part of any mobile app. A well-designed user interface can make an app more accessible, intuitive, and engaging for users. Kivy provides a range of tools and widgets that can be used to create visually appealing and interactive user interfaces.

Kivy's user interface toolkit is designed to work with touch screens and supports a range of input events, including multi-touch and gestures. This allows developers to create user interfaces that are responsive and intuitive to use. Kivy also provides a range of customizable widgets that can be used to create unique app designs.

When designing a mobile app's user interface, developers must consider platform-specific design guidelines. For example, iOS has specific design guidelines that differ from Android. Developers must also consider the device's screen size and resolution, as this can affect how the user interface is displayed.

Mobile App Deployment with Python

Deploying a mobile app involves making the app available to users. Python developers can deploy their mobile apps through various methods, such as app stores, standalone installers, or web-based app platforms.

App stores, such as Google Play and the Apple App Store, are the most common method for distributing mobile apps. App stores provide a centralized location for users to download and install apps. Python developers must follow the app store's guidelines and ensure that their apps meet the store's requirements for quality and security. Python developers can use the Kivy Buildozer tool to package their code into a standalone APK or IPA file, which can then be submitted to app stores.

Standalone installers can also be used to distribute mobile apps. A standalone installer is a file that contains all the necessary files and libraries needed to run the app. Python developers can use tools such as PyInstaller to create standalone installers for their mobile apps.

Web-based app platforms, such as Progressive Web Apps (PWAs), are another option for deploying mobile apps. PWAs are web apps that provide a native app-like experience on mobile devices. PWAs can be accessed through a web browser and can be installed on the device's home screen, providing users with quick access to the app. Python developers can use web frameworks such as Flask or Django to build PWAs.

When deploying mobile apps, developers must consider the app's security and performance. Mobile apps must be secure to protect user data and prevent unauthorized access. Python developers can use security libraries such as PyCryptodome or cryptography to ensure their apps are secure.

Mobile app performance is also crucial, as users expect apps to load quickly and run smoothly. Python developers can optimize their code and use performance analysis tools, such as PyCharm or Visual Studio Code, to ensure their apps run smoothly.

Python's versatility, simplicity, and cross-platform capabilities make it an excellent choice for mobile app development. The Kivy library provides developers with a range of tools and widgets to create visually appealing and interactive user interfaces. Python's cross-platform capabilities allow developers to write code once and deploy it on multiple platforms, reducing development time and costs.

When developing mobile apps with Python, developers must consider the platform-specific design guidelines and ensure their apps meet the app store's quality and security requirements. Python developers can deploy their mobile apps through various methods, such as app stores, standalone installers, or web-based app platforms.

Python is a powerful tool for mobile app development that provides developers with a range of libraries and frameworks to create high-quality mobile apps. With the Kivy library and Python's cross-platform capabilities, developers can create visually appealing and interactive mobile apps that work on various operating systems.

Exercises

1. Build a simple cross-platform mobile app with Kivy
2. Create user registration and login screens with Kivy
3. Design animations and UI transitions for mobile apps with Kivy
4. Integrate live camera feed into a Kivy mobile application
5. Develop mobile games using Kivy like pong, brick breaker etc
6. Build location-based apps with GPS, Maps and Kivy
7. Incorporate biometric authentication like fingerprint scan into a Kivy app
8. Create database backend with SQLite for mobile app data
9. Debug and performance test a Kivy mobile application
10. Distribute mobile apps on Play Store and App Store using Buildozer

Chapter 5 : Real-world Projects and Case Studies

Developing a Web Application

Python is commonly used to build web applications due to its extensive libraries, simple syntax, and cross-platform capabilities. Web frameworks like Django and Flask provide structure and tools for handling routing, templating, databases, authentication, and more. In this section, we will build a simple web app using Flask to demonstrate common workflows like setting up the project, defining routes and views, integrating a database, and deploying the app. Readers will learn best practices for structuring Flask apps and gain hands-on experience to create their own web applications.

Flask Overview

Flask is a popular, lightweight Python web framework. Here are some key features:

- Minimalist and flexible - Easy to get started, but extensible
- Built-in development server and debugger
- Integrates with libraries like Jinja for templating
- Supports extensions for add-ons like database integration

Project Setup

To set up a Flask project, we first create a project directory and initialize Git for version control:

```
 code
$ mkdir myproject
$ cd myproject
$ git init
```

Next we'll create a virtual environment to isolate our dependencies:

```
 code
$ python3 -m venv venv
$ . venv/bin/activate
```

Now we can install Flask and any other libraries we need:

```
 code
$ pip install flask
$ pip install flask-sqlalchemy flask-migrate
```

We initialize Flask by creating an app.py file:

```
python
 code
```

```
from flask import Flask
app = Flask(__name__)


@app.route('/')
def index():
    return 'Hello, World!'


if __name__ == '__main__':
   app.run(debug=True)
```

This creates the Flask app instance and a simple route. We can run the dev server:

```
 code
$ python app.py
* Running on http://localhost:5000/
```

And view our app in the browser. Let's build this out into a real web app.

Defining Routes

Flask uses the @app.route decorator to bind functions to URLs. We can define multiple routes to handle each page:

```
python
 code
@app.route('/')
def index():
   return 'Welcome!'


@app.route('/about')
def about():
   return 'About me page'
```

```
@app.route('/contact')
def contact():
   return 'Contact page'
```

Rendering Templates

Instead of returning simple strings, we can render templates using the render_template() function:

```
python
 code
from flask import render_template

@app.route('/')
def index():
    return render_template('index.html')

@app.route('/about')
def about():
    return render_template('about.html')
```

Flask will look for the templates in a templates folder.

Static Files

For CSS, JS, and images, Flask can serve static files from a folder called static:

```
python
 code
from flask import url_for

@app.route('/about')
def about():
    return render_template('about.html')
```

```
# Link CSS file in template
<link rel="stylesheet" href="{{ url_for('static',
filename='style.css') }}">
```

Handling Forms

To handle form submissions, we use request.form:

```
python
 code
from flask import request

@app.route('/contact', methods=['GET', 'POST'])
def contact():
    if request.method == 'POST':
        name = request.form['name']
        email = request.form['email']
        # Process form data
        ...
    return render_template('contact.html')
```

In the template, we create the form with the name attributes:

```
html
 code
<form method="POST">
    <input name="name">
    <input name="email">
    <input type="submit">
</form>
```

Database Integration

Flask can integrate with databases like SQLite and PostgreSQL using Flask-SQLAlchemy. First we initialize the database:

```
python
 code
from flask_sqlalchemy import SQLAlchemy


app = Flask(__name__)
db = SQLAlchemy(app)


class User(db.Model):
    id = db.Column(db.Integer, primary_key=True)
    username = db.Column(db.String(80), unique=True,
nullable=False)
    email = db.Column(db.String(120), unique=True,
nullable=False)
```

This creates a User model. We can then query the database:

```
python
 code
@app.route('/')
def index():
    users = User.query.all()
    return render_template('index.html', users=users)
```

And pass the data to templates to generate HTML.

Deployment

To deploy, we first create a Procfile for our app:

```
 code
```

```
web: gunicorn app:app
```

We can then use a service like Heroku to deploy from Git:

```
code
$ git push heroku main
$ heroku ps:scale web=1
```

This pushes our code and starts the web process. Our app is now live on production!

We've covered the key steps and best practices for writing a Flask web application. Readers can use this foundation to start building their own real-world web apps.

Data Analysis and Visualization Project

Python is a popular choice for data analysis because of its powerful libraries like Pandas, NumPy, and Matplotlib. In this section, we'll walk through a sample data science project to demonstrate common workflows like loading data, cleaning and processing, applying analysis and machine learning algorithms, and creating visualizations. Readers will gain practical experience in order to use Python for their own data projects.

Project Overview

We will build a data analysis project to predict house sale prices based on attributes like square footage, number of bedrooms, location, etc. Here are the key tasks:

- Load and explore the raw dataset
- Clean the data by handling missing values, formatting, etc.
- Derive new features from existing columns
- Apply algorithms to fit and evaluate machine learning models

- Use visualizations to inspect the data
- Interprete the results and identify insights

Loading Data

We'll use a CSV dataset from Kaggle. First we import Pandas to load the data into a DataFrame:

```
python
 code
import pandas as pd


df = pd.read_csv('housing.csv')
```

Now df contains our data with each row as a record and columns as attributes.

Exploring Data

Let's explore the DataFrame to understand the data better. We can check:

- Size - df.shape
- Column names - df.columns
- Sample rows - df.head()
- Stats on columns - df.describe()
- Missing values - df.isnull().sum()

This gives us a high-level view of the data and identifies any issues to address during cleaning.

Data Cleaning

We prepare the raw data for analysis by:

- Handling missing values using fillna(), dropna() etc.
- Fixing formatting errors and inconsistencies
- Converting data types using astype()
- Parsing dates with to_datetime()
- Normalizing columns like zipcode for consistency

```
python
 code
# Fill NA values
df['lot_size'] = df['lot_size'].fillna(df['lot_size'].
median())
# Convert to proper datatype
df['sqft'] = df['sqft'].astype(int)
# Normalize zipcode
df['zipcode'] = df['zipcode'].apply(lambda x: x[:5])
```

Feature Engineering

We can derive new insightful features from existing columns:

```
python
 code
# Add column for price per sqft
df['price_per_sqft'] = df['price'] / df['sqft']
# Add column for house age
df['age'] = 2022 - df['year_built']
```

These engineered features will help our models.

Model Training

We can explore different machine learning algorithms like linear regression, random forest, SVM, etc. to fit a model predicting house prices. First we split data into train and test sets:

```
python
 code
from sklearn.model_selection import train_test_split


X = df.drop('price', axis=1)
y = df['price']


X_train, X_test, y_train, y_test = train_test_
split(X, y, test_size=0.3, random_state=42)
```

Then we train a model on the data:

```
python
 code
from sklearn.linear_model import LinearRegression


model = LinearRegression()
model.fit(X_train, y_train)
```

And evaluate on the test set:

```
python
 code
from sklearn.metrics import r2_score, mean_squared_
error


predictions = model.predict(X_test)


rmse = mean_squared_error(y_test, predictions)
```

```
r2 = r2_score(y_test, predictions)

print(rmse)
print(r2)
```

We continue exploring different algorithms and hyperparameters to improve accuracy.

Data Visualization

We can use Matplotlib and Seaborn to visualize the data for insights. For example:

```
python
 code
# Histogram of house prices
import matplotlib.pyplot as plt
plt.hist(df['price'])
plt.show()
# Heatmap of correlations
import seaborn as sns
sns.heatmap(df.corr(), annot=True)
plt.show()
```

Visualizations reveal relationships and patterns to help guide the analysis.

This covers the core workflow for a Python data analysis project. Readers can use these steps on their own data to extract insights.

Automation Scripts and Tools

Python is well-suited for writing automation scripts and tools to handle repetitive tasks. The standard library and vast ecosystem provide modules to integrate with the OS, file system, networks, emails, APIs, databases, GUIs, and more. In this section, we will build a few sample automation scripts to demonstrate Python's capabilities for task automation, system administration, and increasing productivity. Readers will learn techniques they can apply to automate common workflows.

Web Scraping

Web scraping extracts data from websites using Python. We can scrape data into structured formats like JSON or CSV for further analysis. Here is an example using BeautifulSoup to scrape a table:

```
python
 code
from bs4 import BeautifulSoup
import requests


URL = 'https://example.com/table'


resp = requests.get(URL)
soup = BeautifulSoup(resp.content, 'html.parser')
table = soup.find('table', {'id': 'data'})


headers = []
for th in table.find('tr').find_all('th'):
    headers.append(th.text.strip())


rows = []
for tr in table.find_all('tr')[1:]:
   data = []
   for td in tr.find_all('td'):
       data.append(td.text.strip())
   rows.append(data)
```

```python
import pandas as pd
df = pd.DataFrame(rows, columns=headers)
# Export to CSV
df.to_csv('data.csv', index=False)
```

The scraped data is now in a structured CSV that can be analyzed.

File Processing

Python lets us automate bulk file processing tasks like:

- Rename files based on patterns
- Move files into categorized folders
- Apply filters like image resizing
- Extract file metadata like EXIF data
- Transcode video and audio files

Here is an example script to rename image files:

```python
python
 code
import os
from PIL import Image

for f in os.listdir('.'):
    if f.endswith('.jpg'):
        image = Image.open(f)
        metadata = image.metadata
        date = metadata['DateTime']
        name = date.replace(':', '-') + '.jpg'
        os.rename(f, name)
```

This simplifies the tedious task of manually renaming many images.

Excel Automation

Python can automate Excel using the OpenPyXL library:

```
python
 code
import openpyxl


wb = openpyxl.load_workbook('data.xlsx')
# Read cell values
print(wb['Sheet1']['A1'].value)
# Update values
wb['Sheet1']['B1'] = 'Updated value'
# Save workbook
wb.save('updated.xlsx')
```

We can use these capabilities to programmatically update Excel reports, consolidate data from multiple sheets, apply formulas, create charts, and more.

Email Scripts

Here is an example script to send customized email reminders:

```
python
 code
import smtplib
from email.message import EmailMessage
import csv


with open('emails.csv') as file:
    reader = csv.reader(file)
    next(reader) # Skip header
```

```
for name, email, reminder in reader:
  msg = EmailMessage()
  msg.set_content(f'Hi {name}, {reminder}')

  msg['Subject'] = f'Reminder'
  msg['From'] = 'me@example.com'
  msg['To'] = email

  server = smtplib.SMTP('localhost')
  server.send_message(msg)
  server.quit()
```

The script reads data from a CSV, templates a custom reminder email per row, and sends via SMTP. This automated emails specific to each recipient.

These examples demonstrate Python's broad capabilities for task automation beyond data analysis. Readers can apply these techniques to automate their own common workflows.

Practical Exercise: Building a Project from Scratch

For this exercise, readers will get hands-on practice developing a Python project from scratch. We will build a simple command line application to manage a to-do list. Readers are encouraged to follow along to reinforce their understanding of the key concepts covered in this chapter.

Project Overview

Our app will allow users to:

- Create new tasks
- Mark tasks as completed
- Delete tasks

- List all tasks

Tasks will be stored in a SQLite database. The app will run via a command line interface.

Set Up Environment

We begin by creating a project folder and virtual environment:

```
code
$ mkdir todo-app
$ cd todo-app
$ python3 -m venv env
$ source env/bin/activate
```

Next we install our dependencies:

```
code
$ pip install click SQLAlchemy dataset
```

- Click provides the CLI interface
- SQLAlchemy interfaces with the database
- Dataset provides convenience functions for working with data

Database Model

We will use SQLite for our database. First we create the database file:

```
code
$ touch database.db
Next we define our table schema:
python
code
from sqlalchemy import Column, Integer, String
from sqlalchemy.ext.declarative import declarative_
```

```
base

Base = declarative_base()

class Task(Base):
    __tablename__ = 'tasks'

    id = Column(Integer, primary_key=True)
    description = Column(String)
    completed = Column(Integer, default=0)
```

This gives us a Task model to represent each to-do item.

Database Setup

Now we can create our database engine and connect to SQLite:

```
python
 code
from sqlalchemy import create_engine

engine = create_engine('sqlite:///database.db')
Base.metadata.create_all(engine)
```

This initializes the database with our tasks table.

Define CLI Interface

We will use Click to create the command line interface. Here are the click commands to handle each action:

```
python
 code
import click
```

```
@click.group()
def cli():
    pass

@cli.command()
@click.argument('description')
def add(description):
    click.echo(f'Added task: {description}')
# Additional commands for list, complete, delete
```

@click.group() creates the entry point, and @cli.command() handles each action.

Integrate Database

Now we integrate SQLAlchemy to save tasks to the database:

```
python
 code
from sqlalchemy.orm import sessionmaker

Session = sessionmaker(bind=engine)
session = Session()

@cli.command()
@click.argument('description')
def add(description):
    task = Task(description=description)
    session.add(task)
    session.commit()
    click.echo(f'Added task: {description}')
```

We reuse this session to query the database for the other actions.

Run the CLI

Finally, we run our CLI app:

```
 code
$ python app.py --help
$ python app.py add "Clean room"
Added task: Clean room
```

This completes our simple todo list manager app! Readers now have direct experience building a Python project end-to-end.

Chapter 6: Future Work and Next Steps

Python is a powerful programming language that is versatile and widely used across a variety of industries. In this book, we have covered the basics of Python, including data types, variables, operators, control flow, functions and modules, input and output, object-oriented programming, and advanced topics like regular expressions, lambda functions, list comprehensions, decorators, generators, and more.

In this chapter, we will summarize the key concepts and techniques covered in this book, and provide tips for continued learning and practice.

Review of Python Basics

Data Types: Python has a number of built-in data types, including integers, floating-point numbers, strings, booleans, and more. These data types can be used to perform mathematical operations, store and manipulate text, and perform logic and comparison operations.

Variables: Variables are used to store data in Python. They can be assigned values and updated as needed. Python has some naming conventions for variables that should be followed to ensure clarity and readability.

Operators: Python has several types of operators, including arithmetic, comparison, logical, and bitwise operators. These operators can be used to perform various operations on data.

Control Flow: Control flow statements like if/else and loops allow you to control the flow of your program. If/else statements are used to make decisions based on conditions, while loops allow you to repeat code until a condition is met.

Functions and Modules: Functions are reusable blocks of code that can be called from other parts of your program. Modules are collections of functions and other code that can be imported into your program to extend its functionality.

Input and Output: Python has several built-in functions for working with input and output, including reading from and writing to the console and working with files.

Object-Oriented Programming: Python supports object-oriented programming, which allows you to create classes and objects to represent real-world concepts in your program. Classes can have methods and attributes, and can be inherited from to create new classes.

Advanced Topics: Python also has several advanced features, such as regular expressions, lambda functions, list comprehensions, decorators, and generators. These features can be used to make your code more concise and efficient.

Tips for Continued Learning and Practice

Now that you have learned the basics of Python programming, it's important to continue practicing and expanding your knowledge. Here are some tips for continued learning and practice:

- Practice regularly: The more you practice coding in Python, the better you will become. Try to set aside a certain amount of time each day or week to practice coding, and challenge yourself with new projects and problems.

- Participate in online communities: There are many online communities and forums where you can connect with other Python programmers and learn from their experiences. Some popular communities include the Python subreddit, Stack Overflow, and GitHub.

- Attend meetups and conferences: Attending in-person meetups and conferences is a great way to network with other Python programmers and learn about new developments in the language. Look for local meetups or larger conferences like PyCon.

- Contribute to open-source projects: Contributing to open-source Python projects is a great way to gain experience working on real-world projects and to learn from other experienced programmers. Look for open-source projects on GitHub or other code hosting platforms.

- Take online courses and tutorials: There are many online courses and tutorials available for Python programming, covering a wide range of topics and skill levels. Some popular online learning platforms include Udemy, Coursera, and Codecademy.

- Read books and blogs: There are many books and blogs available on Python programming, covering everything from basic concepts to advanced topics. Some popular books include "Python Crash Course" by Eric Matthes and "Fluent Python" by Luciano Ramalho.

- Challenge yourself with projects: One of the best ways to learn and practice Python is by working on your own projects. Challenge yourself with new and challenging projects, and don't be afraid to experiment and try new things.

Future Directions and Applications for Python

Python is a versatile programming language that has gained immense popularity over the years. Its user-friendly syntax and extensive libraries make it an ideal choice for developing a wide range of applications. Here are some of the emerging trends and technologies in Python:

- Artificial Intelligence and Machine Learning: Python is widely used in the field of AI and machine learning. With libraries like TensorFlow, PyTorch, and scikit-learn, developers can easily create complex models and algorithms.
- Web Development: Python is also popular for web development, with frameworks like Django and Flask providing a solid foundation for building scalable and robust web applications.
- Data Science: Python is the preferred language for data science and analytics. With libraries like pandas and NumPy, developers can easily manipulate and analyze data.
- Robotics: Python is also gaining popularity in the field of robotics. Its ease of use and versatility make it an ideal language for programming robots.

Applications of Python in different fields:

Python finds applications in a variety of fields due to its flexibility, versatility, and extensive libraries. Here are some of the fields where Python is widely used:

- Web Development: Python is widely used for web development, with frameworks like Django and Flask providing a solid foundation for building web applications.

- Data Science: Python is the preferred language for data science and analytics due to its extensive libraries like NumPy, pandas, and Matplotlib.
- Artificial Intelligence and Machine Learning: Python is widely used for developing AI and machine learning applications. With libraries like TensorFlow, PyTorch, and scikit-learn, developers can easily create complex models and algorithms.
- Scientific Computing: Python is extensively used in scientific computing due to its ease of use and extensive libraries like SciPy, SymPy, and pandas.
- Education: Python is also widely used in education due to its easy-to-learn syntax and versatility. It is used to teach programming concepts and is also used for scientific and mathematical calculations.

Appendix: Python Reference

The Appendix of this book serves as a quick reference guide for Python syntax and features. It is a valuable resource for anyone who wants to quickly look up Python code syntax or find a specific function or module. This section is designed to be used as a reference, not as a tutorial, so it assumes that you have already covered the material in the previous chapters.

Python Version

Python has multiple versions available for use, but the two most commonly used versions are Python 2 and Python 3. It is important to know which version of Python you are using since there are differences in syntax and functionality between the two versions. Python 2 is no longer being developed, and users are encouraged to switch to Python 3.

Syntax

Python syntax is simple and easy to learn. Here are a few basic rules to keep in mind when writing *Python code:*

- Indentation: Python uses whitespace to indicate block-level scoping. Indentations of four spaces or one tab are commonly used to mark indentation levels.
- Comments: Use a hash (#) symbol to start a comment. Comments are ignored by the interpreter.
- Statements: Python code is made up of statements. A statement is a single line of code that performs a specific task.
- Blocks: A block is a group of statements that are executed together.

Data Types

Python has several built-in data types that are used to store and manipulate data. Here are some of the most common data types in Python:

- Numbers: Python supports integer, float, and complex numbers.
- Strings: A string is a sequence of characters, enclosed in either single or double quotes.
- Booleans: A boolean is a value that is either True or False.
- Lists: A list is a collection of items that are ordered and changeable. Lists are created using square brackets.
- Tuples: A tuple is similar to a list, but it is immutable, meaning it cannot be changed after creation. Tuples are created using parentheses.
- Sets: A set is an unordered collection of unique items. Sets are created using curly braces.

- Dictionaries: A dictionary is a collection of key-value pairs. Each key is unique, and the associated value can be of any data type. Dictionaries are created using curly braces.

Variables

Variables are used to store data in Python. A variable is a name that refers to a value. To assign a value to a variable, use the equals (=) operator. Here are a few rules to keep in mind when working with variables:

- Naming conventions: Variable names can contain letters, numbers, and underscores, but they cannot start with a number. Variable names should be descriptive and follow a consistent naming convention.
- Variable assignment: To assign a value to a variable, use the equals (=) operator.
- Variable types: Variables in Python are dynamically typed, meaning that they can hold values of any data type.

Operators

Operators are used to perform operations on data in Python. Python has several built-in operators, including arithmetic, comparison, logical, and bitwise operators. Here are a few examples:

- Arithmetic operators: + (addition), - (subtraction), * (multiplication), / (division), % (modulus), ** (exponentiation)
- Comparison operators: == (equal to), != (not equal to), < (less than), > (greater than), <= (less than or equal to), >= (greater than or equal to)
- Logical operators: and (logical and), or (logical or), not (logical not)
- Bitwise operators: & (bitwise and), | (bitwise or), ^ (bitwise exclusive or), ~ (bitwise)

String Methods

Python provides a variety of string methods that allow you to manipulate and work with strings in a flexible and powerful way. Here are some commonly used string methods:

- .upper() and .lower() : These methods convert a string to all uppercase or lowercase letters, respectively.
- .capitalize() : This method capitalizes the first letter of a string.
- .title() : This method capitalizes the first letter of each word in a string.
- .strip() : This method removes any leading or trailing whitespace from a string.
- .replace(old, new) : This method replaces all occurrences of a substring old with another substring new.
- .split() : This method splits a string into a list of substrings based on a delimiter (default is whitespace).
- .join(iterable) : This method joins the elements of an iterable (such as a list) into a single string, separated by the string on which the method is called.

Date and Time

Python provides a built-in module called datetime that makes it easy to work with dates and times. Here are some of the most commonly used classes and methods in the datetime module:

- datetime.datetime(year, month, day, hour=0, minute=0, second=0, microsecond=0) : This class represents a specific date and time. You can create an instance of this class with the desired date and time values.

- datetime.date(year, month, day) : This class represents a date (without time). You can create an instance of this class with the desired date values.
- datetime.time(hour=0, minute=0, second=0, microsecond=0) : This class represents a time (without date). You can create an instance of this class with the desired time values.
- datetime.datetime.now() : This method returns the current date and time.
- datetime.date.today() : This method returns the current date.
- datetime.timedelta(days=0, seconds=0, microseconds=0, milliseconds=0, minutes=0, hours=0, weeks=0) : This class represents a duration of time. You can create an instance of this class with the desired duration values, and use it to perform arithmetic on datetime objects.

File Handling

- Python makes it easy to read from and write to files. Here are some commonly used file handling functions:
- open(filename, mode) : This function opens a file with the specified name and mode. The mode can be 'r' for reading, 'w' for writing (creating a new file or overwriting an existing file), or 'a' for appending to an existing file. By default, the mode is 'r'.
- .read() : This method reads the entire contents of a file and returns it as a string.
- .readline() : This method reads a single line from a file and returns it as a string.
- .readlines() : This method reads all lines from a file and returns them as a list of strings.
- .write(string) : This method writes a string to a file.

- .writelines(list) : This method writes a list of strings to a file, with each string on a separate line.
- .close() : This method closes a file.

Exception Handling

Sometimes, errors occur in your Python code. Exception handling is a way to handle these errors gracefully, so that your program doesn't crash. Here's how exception handling works in Python:

- try : This keyword starts a block of code that might raise an exception.
- except : This keyword starts a block of code that will be executed if an exception is raised in the preceding try block. finally : This keyword starts a block of code that will be executed whether or not an exception was raised in the preceding try block.

For example, suppose you want to open a file in your Python program. If the file doesn't exist, Python will raise a FileNotFoundError. You can use exception handling to catch this error and handle it gracefully:

try: f = open("myfile.txt", "r") print(f.read()) except FileNotFoundError: print("File not found!") finally: f.close()

In this code, we try to open the file "myfile.txt" for reading, and if an error occurs (such as the file not existing), we catch the FileNotFoundError and print a message saying that the file was not found. Then, we use the finally block to ensure that the file is properly closed, whether or not an exception was raised.

Object-Oriented Programming Python is an object-oriented programming language, which means that it allows you to define classes and objects. A class is a blueprint for creating objects, while an object is an instance of a class. Here's an example of a simple class in Python:

```
class Person: def init(self, name, age): self.name =
```

```
name self.age = age
def greet(self):
    print("Hello, my name is", self.name, "and I am",
self.age, "years old.")
```

In this code, we define a class called "Person" that has two attributes (name and age) and one method (greet). The init method is a special method that gets called when an object is created from the class, and it initializes the object's attributes. The greet method is a simple method that prints a greeting message.

We can create an object of the Person class like this:

```
p = Person("John", 30) p.greet()
```

This code creates a new Person object with the name "John" and age 30, and then calls the greet method on the object, which prints the greeting message.

Exercises

1. Practice Python basics like data types, control structures on practice problems
2. Implement algorithms like sorting, searching and string manipulation
3. Learn object oriented programming concepts like classes, inheritance
4. Work on projects to apply Python to areas like web, data science, ML etc
5. Contribute to open source Python projects on GitHub
6. Attend Python workshops, meetups and conferences to learn from community
7. Stay updated with latest Python trends, libraries and tools

8. Develop expertise in Python web frameworks like Django, Flask
9. Master Python GUI development with PyQt, Tkinter
10. Learn strategies like unit testing, debugging, profiling for robust Python code

Conclusion

In this book, we have covered a wide range of topics related to the Python programming language, from the basics of Python syntax to advanced topics like machine learning and data analysis.

We started with an introduction to Python and its features, followed by a discussion of basic concepts like data types, variables, and control flow. We then moved on to more advanced topics like object-oriented programming, regular expressions, and Python libraries like NumPy and Pandas.

In the later chapters, we explored working with APIs, data analysis and visualization, and machine learning with Python. Finally, we included a comprehensive index to help readers locate specific information easily.

We hope that this book has provided readers with a solid foundation in Python programming and the tools necessary to become proficient in using it. Python is an incredibly versatile and powerful language, and we believe that with the knowledge gained from this book, readers will be able to tackle a wide range of projects and challenges.

Thank you for reading, and we wish you all the best in your Python programming journey!

Made in United States
Troutdale, OR
11/03/2026

56847580R00189